THE MEDIA HANDBOOK

THE
MEDIA
HANDBOOK

Helen Katz

Printed on recyclable paper

NTC Business Books

a division of *NTC Publishing Group* • Lincolnwood, Illinois USA

Library of Congress Cataloging–in–Publication Data

Katz, Helen E.
   The media handbook : a complete guide to advertising, media
selection, planning, research & buying / Helen Katz.
     p.   cm.
   Includes bibliographical references
   ISBN 0–8442–3516–4
   1. Advertising media planning.   2. Mass media and business.
3. Marketing channels. I. Title.
   HF5826.5.K38   1995
   659—dc20   94–23760
                                                      CIP

Published by NTC Business Books, a division of NTC Publishing Group
4255 West Touhy Avenue
Lincolnwood (Chicago), Illinois 60646-1975, U.S.A.

5 6 7 8 9 BC 9 8 7 6 5 4 3 2 1

CONTENTS

Foreword

Hardly a day goes by that we don't read about at least one new development in the media marketplace. It may be a new idea about integrated marketing communications, a new proposed ramp on the interactive superhighway, a new media alliance, a new message delivery system, or a new attempt to measure media effectiveness.

Just as it's getting harder to keep up with the many new developments, it is also getting easier for us to lose sight of the important principles and practices that will always be the key elements of sound media planning and buying.

In my nearly 40 years as a media practitioner, a professor, and a consultant, I have learned that you can't deal with either the old or the new unless you have a solid grasp of the tools, terms, and techniques to do so. Fortunately, Helen Katz (no relationship to Ron Kaatz, even though I'd be proud to claim her) has done it all in *The Media Handbook*. Helen's well-honed skills as a media professional, a researcher, a writer, and a teacher come through loud and clear in her first-rate new book. *The Media Handbook* is a must buy for everyone trying to understand media, plan media, and buy media in our constantly changing marketing communications world.

We've gone through periods when marketing was king and times when creative ruled. I believe that the coming years will find media in charge. And if you want to lead the charge, you will need to be well grounded in everything Helen has to say.

Congratulations to everyone who has already purchased *The Media Handbook!* You're already on the right ramp of the media knowledge superhighway. If you are just paging through a borrowed copy, however, order your very own today. And if you're browsing through *The Media Handbook* at your favorite bookstore, go straight to the cashier and make a very sound investment in your future. Don't leave the store without it!

Ron Kaatz

Associate Professor
Integrated Marketing Communications
Medill School of Journalism
Northwestern University

former Senior Vice President
J. Walter Thompson Company

Preface

"What do you do in media?" I have been asked this question so many times, both by people working in an advertising agency and those in other areas of advertising and marketing. Despite the trend toward teamwork and the breaking down of organizational barriers, it still seems as if, all too often, there is a gulf separating the media planners and buyers from everyone else involved in the marketing process. Account executives deal with the client, creatives design the message, and consumer researchers focus on what people think, feel, and do. Yet somehow, almost by magic, the brand's message appears on television or radio, in magazines or newspapers, on billboards or buses. How did it get there? What was the rationale and the strategic thinking behind it? How will it help sell more widgets?

All of these questions are answered in *The Media Handbook.* As the title suggests, it is designed as a basic introduction to the media planning and buying process, taking the reader through the work of the person we have chosen to call the *media specialist,* from defining the marketing and advertising objectives to execution of the buys and post-buy follow up. While each chapter is almost worthy of a book in its own right, the emphasis here is on a clear, concise, and simple explanation of all of the major elements involved in media planning. Media terms are defined when they are introduced so that, in the jargon-filled worlds of media acronyms, the reader will start to feel more comfortable in subsequent discussion of GRPs, DMAs, or BDIs. The book also includes numerous examples, both of actual national brands and local, fictitious products and services in order to provide a better sense of how media planning and buying work in the real world. At the end of the book, a selection of key resources is offered as an appendix for those individuals or companies that wish to find out more about a particular service or system.

Media planning is not, and should not be thought of as, a mystical, incomprehensible process. It certainly involves a good deal of expertise and intelligent thinking, and also requires a judicious combination of art and science, creativity and mathematical applications, but it should be fairly easy to understand by anyone involved in the marketing of a product or service. Indeed, it should really be a prerequisite that all those who are trying to sell something, whether it is a widget or an image, should have the basic knowledge of how media planning operates. That is where the message ends up, and if it is placed incorrectly or not seen by the chosen target audience, even the most creative or inspiring ad will be unable to boost sales.

After reading *The Media Handbook*, you will, I hope, be able to answer the question of what is done in media with confidence, clarity, and a fuller understanding of how media fits in to the larger advertising and marketing picture.

Acknowledgments

This book could not have been written without the assistance and cooperation of many people. First, I must thank my colleagues at DDB Needham Worldwide, who encourage and support my continued desire to undertake projects that are not directly related to my day-to-day responsibilities. Mike White, David Drake, and Beth Uyenco have been particularly supportive. They have also taught me a great deal about the media planning process as it operates in the real world, rather than in the classrooms and textbooks of colleges and universities. Mike's emphasis on seeing the big picture, David's enormous and unending creativity, and Beth's clear and effective pragmatism have all helped me to gain a greater understanding of the advertising and media planning processes. My first boss at the agency, Kevin C. Killion, continues to be a much-valued mentor, with his infectious enthusiasm for media and his refreshing insights into taxing research issues. In addition, I must thank others who helped me with various sections of this book. At DDB Needham, Lisa Blatt and Tina John provided insights and guidance on the local media buying process, while Nancy Evelyn of Cramer-Kresselt Chicago taught me more about the national TV buying arena.

My background in advertising education not only taught me about media planning in the classroom, it also allowed me to work with several individuals whose work and dedication have inspired me. At the University of Illinois, Kim Rotzoll, Steve Helle, and Kent Lancaster (now at the University of Florida) were teachers, advisors, and friends; and in my first teaching position at Michigan State University, Bruce Vanden Bergh encouraged me to try new approaches to teaching media. Their influences on this book may be indirect, but they are certainly very real.

The people at NTC have been both patient and supportive, hanging in with me throughout what turned out to be a much longer writing process than originally intended. In particular, I appreciate all of the help and support given by my editor, Anne Knudsen, as well as the friendly reminders from her assistant editor, Betsy Lancefield.

I could not have completed this text without the support, encouragement, and friendship of my husband, Eric. Although he sometimes thinks the things I do are crazy, he is always there to help me do them. And finally, it was during my maternity leaves for my two daughters, Stephanie and Caroline, that much of this book was written. It is therefore to them that I dedicate this book.

Dedication

To Stephanie and Caroline, who bring sunshine into my life.

Introduction

This book is deliberately designed as a Media Handbook. It will not tell you every last detail about each individual medium, nor will it go into great depth on non-media advertising elements, such as the creative message or the consumer research that goes on behind the scenes. What it will do, however, is give you a complete picture of how media planning, buying and research work. You will see what each function entails, and how they fit together with each other and within the framework of the marketing mix. You will know enough by the end of this book to be able to create your own media plan, or undertake a print or broadcast buy. Even if you are not directly responsible for either of those tasks, a greater understanding of how media fit in to the marketing picture will help you communicate with those who do such work. Each chapter builds on and works off the preceding ones, although once you have been through them all, it is designed to be very easy for you to refer to specific tasks or concepts at a later date. At the end of each chapter you will see a checklist of questions that you should ask yourself if you actually have to fulfill the objective of that particular chapter (such as setting objectives, or evaluating the plan). At the end of the book, you will find a list of additional resources you can turn to for help in media planning, buying, and research.

CHAPTER ONE

What is Media?

I t's 7:30 A.M. You wake up and turn on the radio, then open your local newspaper to see what has been happening in the world. During breakfast you turn on the television to catch a few minutes of the morning news shows. On the subway to work you listen to the local station on your radio, looking out of the window at a few outdoor billboards on the highway that you pass by.

In that brief timespan, you have been immersed in the world of media. Very broadly, that world includes radio, television, newspapers, magazines, and outdoor billboards. Although you selected the radio to listen to music, or the newspaper to read the latest news, or the television to watch a program, what you also did was receive information through a means of communication, or a *medium*. Given this broad definition, you can see that there are in fact hundreds of different media available, such as direct mail, skywriting, coupons, stadium signs, key-rings, and food containers. All of these, and many other media, offer us ways of communicating information to an audience. As advertising media professionals, we are interested in looking at the media as a means of conveying a specific kind of information—an *advertising message*—about a product or service to consumers.

The media play a very important role in our lives. Media help fulfill two basic needs—they *inform* and they *entertain*. We turn to the media when we want to hear the latest world news or what happened in financial markets, for instance. We also look to the media to fill our evenings and weekends with escapist fare to get us out of our everyday, humdrum routine. So television entertains us with movies, dramas, comedies, and sports. Radio offers us a wide variety of music and entertainment to listen to. We turn to magazines to keep up with our favorite hobbies and interests. Newspapers help us keep up with the world around us.

The media's informational role is perhaps best illustrated by considering what happens during a national or international crisis, such as the 1991 Persian Gulf War or the 1992 Los Angeles riots. On each occasion, millions of people were glued to their television sets, tuned in to their radios, and reading newspapers and magazines for daily in-depth coverage and subsequent follow-up stories.

The media also affect our lives through their entertainment function. Television situation comedies such as "All in the Family" and "Mary Tyler Moore" not only reflected what was happening in U.S. society in the 1970s, but also helped to influence attitudes and behaviors concerning the issues of race and equality. Stories appearing in magazines such as *People* or *Life* let us know what is happening in other people's lives, both famous and ordinary. And we take our radios with us to the beach or park so that we can listen to live sports coverage while we relax.

What Media Are Out There?

The world of media can be very broadly divided into two types—print and electronic. Print media include magazines and newspapers, while electronic media cover radio and television. Other media types are not quite so easily categorized. Thus outdoor billboards are generally defined as a *print* medium, while computer services such as Prodigy or CompuServe are labeled as *electronic*. Exhibit 1.1 provides a list of each type.

EXHIBIT 1.1   Major Print & Electronic Media

Print Media	*Electronic Media*
Magazines—Consumer, Farm, Business	Radio—Network, Spot
Newspapers—National, Local	Television—Broadcast, Cable, Spot, Syndication
Outdoor Billboards	Online Services
Yellow Pages	
Direct Mail	

The Role of Media in Business

It is important to emphasize here that the focus of this book is commercial media. That is, the communications media we will be talking about are not there simply to beautify the landscape or fill up the pages of a newspaper. They are designed to sell products to customers. Of course, there are also media that convey information but are not commercial in intent. *Consumer Reports* is a magazine that does not carry any advertising. Neither does public television (except for sponsorships, which we'll talk about later). The white pages of the telephone directory, computer bulletin boards, and airline safety instructions are all informative yet are not advertisements. And books certainly communicate information to their readers. Here, however, we shall concentrate on those media that currently accept advertising messages. It is worth emphasizing the word *currently*. Twenty-five years ago, you did not find commercial messages at supermarkets, schools, doctors' offices or ski slopes. Today, advertisers can reach people in all of those places. Some books now even have corporate "sponsors," who place advertising messages within the pages of the text. In the 1980s, Whittle Communications experimented with publishing slim books of this kind by famous authors, sponsored by companies such as FedEx. While this venture did not succeed, that does not mean another such venture will not be tried again in the future. For what is true for today may very well change by tomorrow.

The generic term *media* (or *medium* in the singular) means different things to different people. To Joe Smith sitting at home on a Friday evening, the "media" mean whatever TV shows he watches or magazines he leafs through. For the Fast-Print copy shop, the media provide a way to advertise this week's special deal on copies. And the Podunk Electric Utility Company uses the media to remind its customers that they can get free replacement lightbulbs.

Strictly speaking, a "medium" may be defined as a means by which something is accomplished, conveyed, or transferred. This deliberately broad definition means that consumer media would cover everything from handbills passed out in parking lots to "For Sale" signs taped to lampposts to the 10-page advertising supplement that fell out of the last copy of *Business Week* you read, to electronic flashing signs in Times Square. The list goes on and on. In the business world, we think of a medium as a way to transfer and convey information about goods or services from the producer to the consumer, who is a potential buyer of that item. There are various ways to accomplish that in business besides using radio, television, or magazines. Product or company publicity, sales brochures, or exhibits can all be useful ways of conveying information to potential buyers. You should note that throughout this book, we will refer to all potential buyers as "consumers."

The Role of Media in Consumers' Lives

As our lives grow increasingly busy and demanding, and as technology moves ahead with ever-more sophisticated ways to improve our lives, it seems that the media are playing a more and more important role in what we do, where we go, or how we behave. As the example at the opening of this chapter suggested, many of us wake up to the sound of the clock-radio; we read the newspaper while watching morning television and eating breakfast. We commute to work either in the car with the radio on, or on the bus or train surrounded by posters with advertising messages on them (or listen to a portable radio during the commute). At work, it is likely there is a radio on during the workday, while many of us watch (or videotape) our favorite soap operas at lunchtime. When we get home in the evening, we'll probably turn on the TV to catch the local news, and after dinner we'll forget about our daily worries by watching some prime-time TV and catching up with the daily newspaper. Before we go to sleep for the night, we'll probably glance through a couple of magazines while lying in bed.

When you sit down to watch TV and see a commercial which then appears in the magazine you are browsing through and is mentioned again in that night's evening newscast because of the tie-in to a local charity event, you generally don't think about the effort that went into coordinating all of those elements. In fact, if the "seams" between them are too obvious, then something probably isn't working right! While you, as a member of the reading or listening or viewing audience, are interested primarily in the particular program or publication, the medium is interested in you as a potential buyer, offering you up to advertisers who wish to talk to you.

The role of media in conveying information through advertising messages is not something consumers generally consider. Indeed, when they do think about it they are likely to complain about being inundated by commercial messages! Yet despite the fact that no one has yet proven "how advertising works," businesses continue to believe in its power, as evidenced by the $138 billion spent in this country on advertising in 1993.

How Media Work with Advertising

Advertising in the media performs the dual role of informing and entertaining. It informs us of the goods and services that are available for us to purchase and use. And, along the way, it often entertains us with some humorous, witty, or clever use of words and pictures. For example, let's say you have invented a new kind of liquid cleanser called *Super-Kleen* that removes stains from furniture. You've shown it to some friends and neighbors, all of whom are convinced that it would be extremely useful to many people. And, from conversations with a local manufacturer, you believe you could arrange for a nearby factory to produce this solution in large quantities. Now, however, the question arises of what to do next. How do you inform people you don't know personally about this wonderful new product?

This is where the media can help. You could place an advertisement in a local newspaper or magazine, or perhaps buy some time on the local radio or TV station. Your message, that "*Super-Kleen* cleans super fast*", would then be disseminated to an audience of hundreds, or possibly thousands, depending on your location.

You might also generate additional publicity by grabbing the attention of a local newspaper reporter who calls you up and wants to write an article on your new invention. Or perhaps you would decide to send personal letters to several influential furniture designers in the area, offering them a free sample in exchange for their opinion of the product. Whatever form of communication you use, all involve sending a message through a medium of one kind or another.

Media advertising also performs another vital function. It helps offset the cost of the media communication itself to consumers. If we did not have commercials on television or radio, the cost of programming would have to come through sponsorships, taxes, or government monies. Public broadcasting in the United States derives most of its income through semi-annual pledge drives, during which viewers and listeners are asked to give money to pay for the services. Government funding provides additional revenues. But even here, more and more public broadcasting television stations are accepting restricted forms of paid commercials as long as they are image-oriented and not hard-sell. Indeed, there is even a network available, Public Broadcasting Marketing, to help advertisers place their spots on public TV stations across the country.

In thinking about the relationship between media and advertising, remember that the media are not limited to magazines, newspapers, or TV. Public relations efforts such as news releases or open houses, or promotions such as rebates or contests are all viable media. Ideally, when advertising is placed in any or all of these media options, the consumer (audience) is surrounded by an integrated and consistent message wherever he or she turns. So in trying to promote your *Super-Kleen* cleaner, your TV ads or outdoor billboards can show people what the product looks like and demonstrate how it works. Then, you might sponsor a local home design seminar as a public relations effort to heighten awareness of the new product, sending out press releases in advance to notify the media of the event and thereby generating additional publicity both for the seminar and for your invention. You could offer retailers a special deal, such as contributing funds to the ads that they run (an advertising allowance), if they will promote the cleanser in their weekly newspaper ads. You might also arrange for brochures to be handed out in stores so that people can learn more about *Super-Kleen*. By advertising the cleanser in a wide variety of media, each one fulfills a slightly different role, but your overall message—that "*Super-Kleen* cleans super fast"—is conveyed clearly and consistently.

Tasks in Media

The broad field of advertising media can be broken down into three primary tasks:

- Planning how to use media to convey the advertising message (the *media planner*)
- Buying media space and time for the message (the *media buyer*)
- Selling that space or time to the advertiser (the *media seller*).

Most large companies handle the media planning and buying functions through an advertising agency. Smaller firms will usually handle this task themselves, through their marketing director, or public relations coordinator. The role of the planner is to decide where and when the message should be placed, how often, and at what cost. The plan is then implemented by the media buyer, who negotiates with the media providers themselves to agree on the space and time needed and to determine or confirm where the ad will appear. That buyer will, of course, be dealing with the salesperson at the media company, whose job it is to sell as much advertising space or time as possible.

Summary

The focus of *The Media Handbook* is the role of media in communicating and conveying information about products and services to potential consumers. It is designed to explore this media world in detail, looking at the various types of communication that are available (printed, aural, visual) and how to use these forms in your day-to-day business. The aim here is to provide a better understanding of what the media are and how they work. There are basically two types of media—print and electronic. Within these categories, consumers choose from a wide array of media in their daily lives, turning to them for both information and entertainment. Advertising in the media also helps to offset the costs of production and distribution. Any company that advertises in the media must deal either directly or indirectly with the planning and buying of advertising space or airtime. This handbook will show you how to do this efficiently and successfully.

CHAPTER TWO

Media in the Marketing Context

Although this book is designed to take the media specialist through the planning and buying of media, those functions do not occur in a vacuum. Both media and advertising are part of the bigger picture of the world of marketing. The primary goal of marketing is to increase sales and profits. To return to our earlier example, where we were wondering how to market our newly invented furniture cleaner, *Super-Kleen,* we had considered many elements beyond which media to use. To market any product effectively involves not simply advertising it, but also figuring out how much to charge for it, where to distribute it, and how to manufacture it. In marketing jargon, these four critical elements are known as the "Four Ps": Product, Price, Place (distribution), and Promotion. Although your job as a media specialist does not necessarily involve making the decisions on all of these criteria, it is critical that you have a clear understanding of how they work, and more importantly, how they can impact your media decisions and strategy. This chapter will guide you through these four marketing basics.

In order to sell anything you must first have a *product* or service. You have to decide how much you need to charge for it (the *price*) so that you can make a profit. You must also figure out how and where the product will be made available to people (*place*, or distribution). And last, but not least, you must consider how you will let potential buyers know what you are offering (*promotion*). Within that last category, there are several key channels of communication: advertising, personal selling, sales promotion, direct marketing, event marketing, and publicity. All can be thought of as media, or ways of conveying information to potential buyers. You can see how these elements work in Exhibit 2.1.

EXHIBIT 2.1   The Marketing Mix

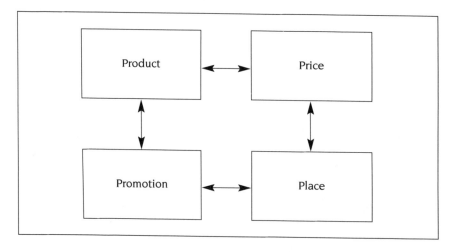

One of the most important things to remember here is that the arrows move in both directions. Almost any decision you make concerning media will have an impact on something else in the marketing mix. For example, if you decided to advertise on network television, you would have to ensure that your product was in fact available throughout the country. Or if you chose to concentrate your advertising efforts during holiday periods (Memorial Day, Fourth of July, and so on), you might consider lowering your price at that time to boost sales even further.

The task of the media planner is to consider all of the marketing information available on the product and use that information to determine how best to reach the target audience through advertising media. In this way, the media plan can be thought of as the pivot point, or hub of the overall marketing plan.

EXHIBIT 2.2   Moving Towards the Media Plan

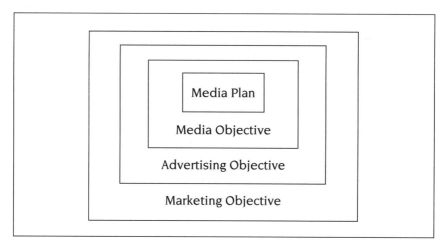

Getting to Know the Consumer

One of the most important pieces of information that marketing can provide for you as a media specialist is an understanding of how your consumers view and use your product or service. To do this you must know more about the brand and the product category. A *brand* is the individual product or service that you are trying to sell. It can be thought of as the name on the label. So Campbell's Tomato soup is a brand, as is their Chicken Noodle soup, or their Clam Chowder variety. The *product category* could either be defined as all brands of tomato soup, or all kinds of soup. In the case of a service, such as insurance, the product category could be one type of insurance, such as life or home or auto, or all types. The brand would be one particular company such as Allstate Insurance, or State Farm.

One way to think about brands is to consider your own behavior. When you go to the grocery store, you are usually not thinking in terms of *product categories* or *brands*. More likely, you are thinking about buying a carton of Yoplait yogurt, three Lean Cuisine frozen dinners, or a box of Wheaties cereal. Similarly, when you have to decide which restaurant to go to, you will not categorize them the way marketers do, into quick-service, family-style, or steak-houses, but will instead think in terms of the types of food—Chinese, Mexican, Indian, etc. And within those groups, you will probably categorize them by geography, thinking of the specific restaurants by area.

What we need to know as marketers and media specialists, however, is how the consumer decides *which* brands and products to buy, as well as the process he or she goes through when purchasing an item. This will vary, depending on the type of product. While a consumer might pick up any brand of paper for her copy machine, the decision process she goes through to select the copier itself is likely to take far longer because there are more elements to consider. Understanding these decision processes will help you decide which media might best be used both to reach your target and convey the desired message. For selling your brand of copy paper, you could probably use a traditional medium such as trade magazines to increase awareness of your brand name. A copier company, however, is likely to use direct marketing and trade promotion techniques such as bind-in cards in trade magazines or co-op advertising encourage its dealers and salesforce to sell the product.

Here, we will take a general look at how consumers view and use brands. From there, we can establish some foundations for the media plan. We will do this by going back into the past and looking at what has happened in the marketplace both to the brand and the product category in which we are interested.

In looking at how consumers use brands, we must answer two key questions: how much do consumers already know about the brand (brand and advertising awareness)? And when, where, and how often do they buy it (purchase dynamics)?

What Do People Know About the Brand?

People have the opportunity to be exposed to at least 2,000 ads every week, so it isn't surprising that they don't remember many of them. In fact, an annual study conducted by the Newspaper Association of

America shows that the percentage of people who can accurately remember the name of the brand they last saw advertised on television has fallen to an all-time low of 4 percent of those surveyed. And although we talk about "great" ads that we saw on television last night, or read in a newspaper or magazine, we are probably unlikely to remember the brand which was being advertised. Does Ray Charles advertise Coca-Cola or Pepsi? Is Michael Jordan the spokesman for Reebok or Nike athletic products? In today's increasingly competitive marketing climate, consumers are also likely to be exposed to more than one brand name in an ad. This *comparison advertising* is extremely common in categories such as analgesics, automobiles, and detergents. But while your brand, Brand A, emphasizes how much better it is than Brand B, will your target audience remember A or B?

How the Media Specialist Gets to Know Consumers

Finding out how aware your consumers are of your brand and its advertising is quite straightforward, though not without pitfalls. The easiest way to do this is through a survey (mail, telephone, or in person), in which you simply ask people what they remember about certain ads. You can do this in one of two ways—either *unaided,* where no prompts or assistance are provided, or *aided,* where you offer some kind of memory aid, such as mentioning something from the advertisement or giving an actual list of brand names and asking for further information on the advertising. The *unaided* method demands more on the part of consumers, asking them to tap deeper into their memories to *recall* the information you are seeking. With the *aided* method, you are basically asking people to recognize a brand and/or advertisement when it is placed before them, and then prompting them for additional information about it.

There are other issues to keep in mind with brand-awareness research. The most important is that you cannot expect complete accuracy. That is, there is always the danger with any kind of memory check that you will not get full information from the people you survey. Obviously, the longer the time between when people see an ad and when they are questioned about it, the less they will remember about it. Human memory is highly fallible. They may attribute pieces of one ad to another ad, or recite a list of brand attributes from Brand A that really belong to Brand B. So if you do test consumer awareness of your ads, be sure that you keep in mind the possibility of inaccuracies in the responses.

In addition, you must remember that all of these responses are what consumers *claim* to recognize or recall. Even if you give people a questionnaire to fill out on their own they may not put down their real feelings or thoughts. They might not want to offend the interviewer or admit how they really feel, or for whatever reason do not want to tell the truth. For instance, they may have a vague recollection of your brand's name, but write down that they are very familiar with it.

Having said that, awareness checks do play a vital role in letting you know more about how your consumer interacts with the brand and its advertising. If no one can recall your brand name after it has been advertised on television every day for the past year, then you have a problem. It could be the message isn't convincing at all, or it could be you are advertising it in the wrong medium. Perhaps people can recall the brand name very easily but nothing about the advertising has stuck in their minds.

If you want to probe further into people's responses, you can find out more through focus groups, which are groups of five to ten people who are interviewed together by a moderator. They are probed for their beliefs, attitudes, or feelings towards a given brand or product category and its advertising to help in development of the creative message as well as the marketing and media strategy.

The importance of awareness should not be understated. It is commonly accepted that without consumer awareness of your brand, even the most spectacular media plan will be unlikely to generate many sales. People are far more likely to purchase a brand whose name they have heard before than one about which they have no information. For those of you who do not feel qualified to conduct this kind of research on your own, there are many companies that provide this service. Some of the larger ones are listed in the Appendix. Also, many smaller market research companies do recall tests on a routine basis.

The Consumer Decision Process

Many research studies have been conducted over the years to demonstrate the decision process that a consumer typically goes through when buying a routine product. In its simplest form, this process has three steps:

1. Think.
2. Feel.
3. Do.

People must first *think* about the item (i.e., be aware of it and know it exists); they must then develop some kind of attitude or *feeling* towards it (i.e., like it and prefer it over others); and finally they must take some action with regard to it (decide on it, and actually buy it). This latter stage is the *do* part of the model.

The process is actually more involved than this, as we see here.

1. Need.
2. Awareness.
3. Preference.
4. Search.
5. Selection.
6. Purchase.
7. Use.
8. Satisfaction.

To begin with, the consumer must first have a *need* to fulfill. He or she then becomes *aware* of the brands available to satisfy that need. After that, several brands are considered acceptable, and a *prefer*ence developed for one or more of them. The consumer will then *search* for the brand(s) desired, and make a *selec*tion of one over the others. A specific brand is *purchased* and *used*. Finally, the level of *satisfaction* obtained with that purchase will help determine whether that brand is bought on a future occasion. This is discussed in detail in the next chapter.

How the Consumer Buys Products

One of the main drawbacks to using surveys or holding discussions with consumers about how they buy is that they are telling you what they *think* they do which may be very different from what they actually do in real life. So in addition to looking at awareness, or the top of the decision tree, you should also pay attention to what is happening at the bottom of the tree, with the purchase cycle. When are people buying your product? How much is bought? Is there some kind of seasonality to their purchases? All of this information will prove to be critical in planning and buying your media, and will have a major impact on how and when you schedule your ads.

When Do People Buy?

The answer to this question is more complex than it seems at first. You might say "Well, they buy my product all the time." But if you look more closely at purchase behavior you will probably detect some kind of pattern. While people are buying houses "all the time," they are more likely to do so when interest rates are low and prices are depressed. People buy cars "all the time," but sales increase when the new models come into the showrooms in the fall. Even everyday kinds of items have a timing component to purchases. Sales of cheese are higher at the weekends and around paydays because that is when people have more money to go shopping. Moving companies are busiest between May and October because that is when most people change their residence. Greeting card sales go up before every holiday (whether traditional, such as Christmas, or "Hallmark holidays," such as Grandparents Day and Mother-in-Law's Day).

If you know when consumers are most likely to buy your product, you can time your media advertising to take advantage of that purchase cycle. For major purchases in particular, you might also want to consider when people are *thinking about* buying. This might occur several weeks, or even months, before they make the actual purchase. So whereas Mr. and Mrs. Smith might buy a new air conditioner in July, they will probably start to think about which one to get several months prior to that. This provides you with a valuable opportunity to get your brand's message to the Smiths early in their decision-making process.

How Much Do They Buy?

The size of consumer purchases is another important element of the purchase cycle for the media specialist to know. That is, what proportion of your brand's sales comes from each size of the product? If you offer three sizes of plant fertilizer (10-pound, 20-pound, and 40-pound bags), which one is most popular? Do most people buy the largest size, and therefore only pick one up every three months? Or do you sell three times as many small bags, perhaps suggesting that your product is used more by the casual gardener? This kind of information is not only important for production and distribution purposes it can also play a key role in your media planning, for the users of each size are likely to be different kinds of people, with different media habits. The casual gardener who picks up the 10-pound bag could be a young, single, professional living in the city, while those who purchase the large size of fertilizer are more likely to be older adults with children, who live in the suburbs. Young working women prefer to watch programs such as "Murphy Brown" and "Seinfeld," and read *Cosmopolitan* and *Glamour;* older adults are more likely to choose "60 Minutes" and *Reader's Digest.* Based on these differences in media preference, you may well end up with two media plans, one for the occasional purchaser of the smaller bag, and another for the serious gardener.

Exhibit 2.3   MRI Profile of Fertilizer User

Male
Graduated or attended college
Age 35–64
Professional or managerial
Household income $40,000+
North or West United States
Suburban
Married, with children
Own home

Source: Mediamark Research, Inc., 1994.

Looking at the Marketplace

Given what you know about how consumers view and use your brand, the next step for the media specialist is to examine what has been happening to that brand in the marketplace in recent times. Given this information on past efforts to sell your product, you can decide whether to continue along the same path or try something different in terms of your media planning and buying. Examining the marketplace involves doing an analysis of historical data on both the brand and the product category. As the famous philosopher George Santayana said, those who do not learn from the past are condemned to repeat it.

Some of the basic questions the media specialist might ask include the following:

- How long has this brand been available?
- How successful has it been throughout its history?
- How has it been positioned in the past?
- What do you know about the company that makes this brand (whether this is your own, or the firm that produces the brand)?

You might think of this as genealogical work—trying to dig up as much "family background" on the brand as possible. You may find that the company has been in business for 150 years, suggesting possible leverage to be gained by emphasizing in the message the long heritage the brand possesses and placing it in media vehicles that have also been around a long time. Or perhaps the company has been around forever, but is now moving in a different direction, starting to explore new opportunities, suggesting the use of new or different media. The Conagra Company, for example, has its heritage in the meat industry. More recently, its Healthy Choice line of products has grown enormously, expanding out of its original line of frozen entrees into soups and desserts. Yet all of these products might be considered to lie within the original and over-arching purpose of the company: to provide consumers with convenient and healthy food products. But the fact that it is offering new and different products may mean the company is now targeting different groups. This, in turn, may result in a need for more diverse, and/or more selective media. Perhaps its luncheon meats would be advertised in women's service magazines such as *Good Housekeeping* or *Woman's Day,* to reach women who are looking for convenient ways to feed their families; in contrast, its newer Healthy Choice desserts might appear in fitness books such as *Shape* or *Self,* appealing more to young, single women concerned about their weight and nutrition.

What Are the Competitors Up To?

In doing a historical analysis of the brand you must also deal with competitive issues. That is, you should not only explore and uncover as much marketing and media information as possible about your *own* brand, but you also need to do the same for *all* the brands against which you do or plan to compete. The marketing part of these issues may divided into three main areas:

- Product category trends.
- Brand trends and share of market.
- Brand's share of requirements.

Product Category Trends

Whether your brand has been available for half a century, two years, or is about to be launched, one of the most important preplanning considerations for the media specialist is what is happening in your product category. If you are creating a media plan for the manufacturer of a mountain bike, you would want to know whether sales of bicycles are increasing, decreasing, or remaining constant. That will immediately influence your media budget, who you choose to target, and how you go about trying to reach them. In some instances, in order to determine how the category has fared, you will have to decide what your "category" really is. If you are selling an oatmeal cookie, then it might seem obvious that it belongs in the cookie category. But perhaps this is a low-calorie, low-cholesterol cookie which belongs more appropriately in the "diet and health food" classification. Does a yogurt drink fit better into yogurt products or milk drinks? And what about fax paper? Is that in paper products, or with fax machine accessories?

How you define your product category will determine not only your assessment of the strengths or weaknesses of that category, but also the direction and potential marketing and media strategies you employ for your particular brand. To take the fax paper example, if you decide it is part of the paper products category, then you might advertise to administrative workers through magazines such as *Office World News* and *Office Products Dealer.* If you decide your brand fits better within the machine accessories category, then perhaps you will try to reach the machine manufacturers to get them to recommend your brand of paper over the competitors, using media such as trade shows or direct mail to do so. Or you might choose to advertise the product to both target groups using a combination of those media.

There are numerous stories in advertising lore of how the redefinition of a product category gave new life to a moribund product or service. Amtrak had been witnessing declining sales for years as the country's sole passenger train in the face of stiff competition from the airlines. However, by redefining itself in the travel and recreation market instead of merely a method of transportation, the company was able to redirect its marketing and media focus so successfully that sales turned up considerably. Perhaps the most renowned case of redefinition is that of Arm and Hammer Baking Soda. By finding a new use for an established product (keeping refrigerators smelling fresh), the brand in effect positioned itself in two completely distinct categories—baking products and home fresheners. Today, it has a huge market share in the latter category.

Once you have determined to which product category your brand rightfully belongs (or the category to which you wish it to belong), you are then in a position to examine trends in that category. You can do this in one of several ways. You may have access to product category sales from a trade association or manufacturers' group of some kind (such as the Juvenile Products Manufacturers Association if you are marketing children's toys, or the Electronics Industries Association if you are marketing electronics sales). You can often find such data in trade journals in your particular field (such as *Supermarket News* for supermarket food sales or *Chemical Week* for sales of liquid nitrogen). One invaluable source for this type of information is the journal *Sales and Marketing Management,* which comes out several times a year with overall category sales (see Exhibit 2.4). *Advertising Age* also produces an advertising-to-sales ratio in all major product categories annually. In many larger companies, these data are collected routinely within the organization, usually within the marketing department.

In looking at category trends, be careful to look back beyond the past year. In fact, if you can find five to ten years of data, you'll be in a much stronger position to see what the real trends are. Another important point to remember is that there will be many factors to explain the rise or fall of product sales. These trends do not occur in a vacuum.

■ **Intepreting Sales Trends.**   Four factors that help explain sales trends are economic, social, political, and cultural trends. And each will, in turn, influence your media choices. For instance, if you are selling a new high-end video camera (camcorder) with lots of fancy features, the overall health of the economy is going to have a large impact on whether people feel they can afford to spend the money to purchase such a piece of equipment. If you decide that despite the economic downturn you want to emphasize a sophisticated image for your product, aiming it at innovators who always want to buy the latest equipment, then you might use magazines targeted to camera aficionados, such as *Darkroom and Creative Camera Techniques.* If, on the other hand, you choose to emphasize the great value-for-money your camera still represents, you might look to a broader audience and use more popular, broad-based vehicles such as *American Photo* or *Popular Photography.*

Politics can play an important role in the marketing of goods and services. For local cable systems trying to promote themselves to potential cable subscribers, what happens in Washington at the Federal Communications Commission, or in state or local politics will affect what they are allowed to sell and whether consumers are likely to buy the service. The 1992 Cable Act, for example, reinstated some federal and local government restrictions on what cable operators could charge for their service. The gradual but persistent increase in

EXHIBIT 2.4 Examples of Product Category Sales Data

ILLINOIS
POPULATION / **RETAIL SALES BY STORE GROUP**

METRO AREA County / City	Total Population (Thousands)	% of US	Median Age of Pop.	18-24 Years	25-34 Years	35-49 Years	50 & Over	Households (Thousands)	Total Retail Sales ($ Thousands)	Food ($ Thousands)	Eating & Drinking Places ($ Thousands)	General Merchandise ($ Thousands)	Furniture/ Furnish. Apps ($ Thousands)	Automotive ($ Thousands)	Drug ($ Thousands)
				% of Population by Age Group											
CHICAGO-GARY-KENOSHA CONSOLIDATED AREA	*8434.2*	*3.2849*	*32.8*	*10.0*	*17.1*	*22.1*	*24.2*	*3,027.7*	*70,464,364*	*11,491,610*	*7,826,278*	*7,736,270*	*4,173,792*	*13,998,386*	*3,899,296*
DAVENPORT-MOLINE-ROCK ISLAND	**350.6**	**0.1365**	**34.5**	**9.0**	**14.8**	**22.0**	**27.3**	**137.0**	**3,183,758**	**569,317**	**342,923**	**445,855**	**151,553**	**671,877**	**167,814**
Henry	50.4	0.0196	36.7	7.3	13.0	22.0	30.6	19.3	336,059	62,715	30,099	38,019	14,901	93,340	17,172
Rock Island	147.2	0.0573	35.5	9.2	14.3	21.4	29.3	59.2	1,281,416	225,434	162,232	185,376	57,982	240,199	86,243
• Moline	42.8	0.0167	36.2	8.2	14.9	21.6	30.2	18.1	617,608	76,123	80,435	138,093	46,039	69,397	30,007
• Rock Island	40.2	0.0157	35.0	11.9	13.1	19.1	31.0	16.1	241,581	45,098	32,828	25,397	5,599	46,327	19,132
Scott, Iowa	*153.0*	*0.0596*	*32.9*	*9.4*	*15.8*	*22.5*	*24.1*	*59.5*	*1,566,264*	*281,168*	*150,592*	*222,461*	*78,670*	*338,338*	*64,399*
• Davenport	96.7	0.0377	32.3	10.4	16.6	20.5	24.9	37.8	1,138,937	194,997	107,879	164,314	68,377	277,319	49,280
SUBURBAN TOTAL	170.9	0.0684	35.4	7.7	14.1	23.7	26.9	65.0	1,185,632	253,099	121,781	118,051	31,538	252,834	69,395

IDAHO
EFFECTIVE BUYING INCOME

METRO AREA County / City ($ Thousands)	Total EBI	Median Hshld EBI	(A) $10,000-$19,999	(B) $20,000-$34,999	(C) $35,000-$49,999	(D) $50,000 & Over	Buying Power Index
			% of Hshlds by EBI Group				
			A	B	C	D	
BOISE	**4,609,148**	**32,506**	**17.0**	**27.9**	**20.3**	**25.2**	**0.1206**
Ada	3,514,700	34,853	15.3	28.4	21.7	28.7	0.0892
• Boise	2,273,104	33,638	15.8	27.2	20.7	26.9	0.0610
Canyon	1,094,448	27,493	21.3	31.3	18.3	16.4	0.0316
• Nampo	309,431	23,682	25.7	37.9	15.8	11.6	0.0123
SUBURBAN TOTAL	2,026,613	33,428	16.3	27.9	20.9	26.3	0.0475

Source: Reprinted with the permission of *Sales and Marketing Management.*

EXHIBIT 2.4   Examples of Product Category Sales Data *(continued)*

1994 Advertising to Sales Ratios for the 200 Largest
Ad Spending Industries

Industry	SIC no.	Ad dollars as percent of sales	Ad dollars as percent of margin	Annual ad growth rate (%)
Abrasive, asbestos, misc. mnrl	3290	1.1	2.5	2.5
Adhesives and sealants	2891	4.8	12.1	7.5
Agriculture chemicals	2870	1.3	7	-8.1
Agriculture production-crops	1000	2.3	7.1	-1.8
Air cond, heating, refrig eq	3585	1.5	5.9	2.6
Air courier services	4513	1.4	12.3	0.8
Air transport, scheduled	4512	1.4	14.6	2.6
Apparel & other finished prods	2300	5.6	15.4	9.1
Auto and home supply stores	5600	2.2	6.3	11.5
Auto rent & lease, no drivers	7510	2.4	13.3	-1.1
Bakery products	2050	9.9	60.7	-7.5
Beverages	2080	7.5	12.5	6.9
Biological prods, ex diagnostics	2836	1.3	2.3	17.7
Blankbooks, binders, bookbind	2780	3.5	6.9	8
Bldg matl, hardware, garden-retail	5200	3.3	10.2	-0.7
Books: pubg, pubg & printing	2731	3.3	6	5.8
Brdwoven fabric mill, cotton	2211	4	16.2	9
Cable and other pay TV svcs	4841	1.1	1.7	-1.5
Calculate, acct mach, ex comp	3578	1.8	4.2	13.8
Can fruit, veg, presrv, jam, jelly	2033	0.8	3.1	-16.3
Can, frozn presrv fruit & veg	2030	7.1	18.4	4.4
Carpets and rugs	2273	2.4	8.1	-8.9
Catalog, mail-order houses	5961	6.8	17.2	10.8
Chemicals & allied prods-whlsle	5160	3.6	12.9	5.3
Chemicals & allied prods	2800	2.8	6.5	2.5
Cigarettes	2111	4.4	7.9	-2.5
Computer and computer software stores	5734	1.5	25.5	23.1
Computer integrated sys design	7373	1.5	4.1	3
Computer processing, data prep svc	7374	1.4	3.1	4.4
Communications equip., NEC	3669	1.5	3.8	-3
Computer & office equip	3576	1.9	3.4	17.6
Computer peripheral eq, NEC	3577	2.8	7	13.8
Computer storage devices	3572	0.8	3.1	6.4
Computers & software-whlsale	5045	0.5	5.9	14.4
Construction machinery & equip	3531	0.2	0.6	-1.1

Source: *Advertising Age.*

cable rates has caused many consumers to feel dissatisfied with their local operators, so many cable systems now run promotional spots on TV which tout their community service activities or other altruistic behaviors.

Cultural changes, while slower to occur, can also explain movements in product sales that have implications for media planning and buying. This is seen in the growth of ethnic foods, such as Mexican or Chinese dishes. The increasing popularity of different ethnic food products can be attributed in part to the growth of the Hispanic and other immigrant populations in the United States, leading to a greater diversity of cultures that are gradually intermingling and changing cultural tastes and preferences. The marketers of these foods try different ways of reaching their target audiences, through product sampling in stores or sponsorship of community events.

Finally, social changes, which also tend to happen slowly, can ultimately have a major impact on media activities. The cigarette companies of today have a much tougher job selling their product than they did twenty or thirty years ago, primarily because smoking is no longer considered socially acceptable due to the proven health risks it carries. Their task is made more difficult because since 1971 they have been forbidden, by law, from advertising on television at all.

So while you as a media specialist may not have to pinpoint all the reasons behind category trends, it is important for you to gain a broad understanding of what is really happening in the category and not simply limit yourself to whether sales are up or down. Having this additional background information will help you decide which media you can or should be using in your plan.

■ **What Should You Measure?** Another important issue when looking at category trends is deciding which trends you should be measuring. Sales? Units? Volume? The answer to this may ultimately depend on the types of data you are able to obtain, but you need to keep in mind that what seems to be a trend when examining one number may disappear or be reversed if you turn to another. For example, while sales of your screwdrivers could be going up in dollar terms, you may actually be selling fewer units if sales are rising primarily due to price increases (i.e., you make more money on each unit sold, but sell fewer units as a result). When looking at category trends in dollar terms, always remember to factor in the effects of inflation. What may seem to be a 7 percent annual growth rate could turn out to be a 2-to-3 percent rate once inflation has been accounted for. Perhaps the category trend line shows that the number of units of windshield washer fluid sold is declining, but volume is holding steady. This might occur if the unit size has been enlarged, so the same total volume is being sold but in larger bottles. Again, ideally, you want to look at several trend lines using diverse measurements so that you can get an overall picture of what is going on in the category.

Brand Trends

When you turn your attention to individual brands, you perform similar analyses to those done at the category level. This time, however, you focus your attention on specific brand names. The use of the plural here is critical: You are not just looking at how *your* brand has been doing over the past several years, but even more importantly, you need to track how your brand's *competitors* have been faring during that same period. This requires finding the answers to the following questions:

- How many competitors are there?
- How many of these are major, and how many minor? In some categories, where there are just a few players, such as the airline industry, you should probably consider all of them, but in larger categories, such as fast-food restaurants, where myriad companies have offerings, you will do better to pay attention to the ones you believe are your most serious threats. In certain instances, it is a good idea to look at all of the competitors regardless of their size; you may find that the fourth-tier player of three years ago has gradually been gaining market share and is now a far bigger concern. Compaq computers were for several years largely ignored by the likes of IBM or AT&T. Today, however, Compaq is the number-one seller of personal computers.
- How is the category characterized? Is it an oligopoly, where three or four brands define the category, or are there twenty or thirty brands each shouting to be heard?
- How aggressively do the brands in this category compete against one another? For example, is it advertising-driven, or promotion-driven, or does everyone rely heavily on direct mail? You can answer this either from your own experience in the category, or by looking at any available syndicated data on competitive media expenditures.

For *each* competitor (ideally for all of them, but at least for the major ones), you must also find out the following:

- What is the company's financial position? This can be found by looking at stock market information or Standard & Poors reports, where available, or by obtaining a recent issue of the company's annual report.

- How does the competitor position its brand? To determine this, you will have to use your own judgment. Examine the advertising for the brand and see what is being emphasized. Is it similar to your own current efforts, or not? If it is dissimilar, is that because there is an actual difference between the two brands, or do consumers just perceive a distinction between them? And who has the more favorable position?

- How does the competitor promote its brand? Which media are used? How much does the competitor spend to promote its brand? Where and when does it spend its money? The answers to these questions may come from several sources. Many large companies, and/or their agencies, subscribe to Competitive Media Reporting (CMR), the main provider of this type of syndicated data. CMR shows, on a monthly, quarterly, and annual basis, how much money was spent by a brand in each major media category (see Exhibit 2.5). For smaller businesses, you may simply try to keep track yourself of where your competitors' ads are appearing. This is not too difficult if you are dealing with a local product, but gets more complicated the wider the area that you or your competitors try to cover. You can also subscribe to a clipping service which will do the tracking for you (see Appendix for more on this).

- **Share of Market.** Once you have looked at the trends for your brand and its competitors, you must then put that information together and see how your brand is faring in the marketplace. The percentage of total category sales that your brand enjoys is known as the *market share*. You should try to examine how this figure has changed over time. Have you been gaining or losing market share in the past few years? Again, be careful to avoid oversimplifying the picture. It could be that you have been losing market share, but so have your major competitors, because of the entry of several new brands into the category. We can see this in the media arena in television. Whereas ten years ago the three broadcast networks commanded 90 percent of

EXHIBIT 2.5   Sample of CMR Data

Parent Company/Brand	Class Code	10-Media Total	Magazines	Sunday Magazines	Newspapers	Outdoor	Network Television	Spot Television	Syndicated Television	Cable TV Networks	Network Radio	National Spot Radio
Anheuser-Busch Cos Inc												
Adventure Island Amusements & Busch Gdns	G322	147.8	0.0	0.0	0.0	0.0	0.0	147.8	0.0	0.0	0.0	0.0
Adventure Island Amusement Park	G322	52.1	0.0	0.0	0.0	21.3	0.0	30.8	0.0	0.0	0.0	0.0
Anheuser-Busch Beers	F310	11,133.1	0.0	0.0	227.8	1,177.2	3,718.2	3.0	0.0	0.0	0.0	6,006.9
Anheuser-Busch Brewery Tours	G329	9.0	9.0	0.0	0.0	0.0	0.0	0.0	0.0	0.0	0.0	0.0
Anheuser-Busch Cos. Inc Art Prints	G612	41.9	41.9	0.0	0.0	0.0	0.0	0.0	0.0	0.0	0.0	0.0
Anheuser-Busch Cos Inc. Corp PSA	F310-8	361.0	62.0	0.0	0.0	0.0	0.0	268.5	0.0	30.5	0.0	0.0
Anheuser-Busch Cos. Inc. General Promotion	F310-8	11,747.8	403.9	0.0	0.0	0.0	7,458.0	2,590.1	114.5	1,181.3	0.0	0.0
Anheuser-Busch Cos. Sporting Events	F310-8	29.7	0.0	0.0	0.0	0.0	0.0	29.7	0.0	0.0	0.0	0.0
Anheuser-Busch Inc. Corp PSA	F310-8	10,928.4	3,233.9	0.0	0.0	0.0	5,865.3	1,187.7	26.4	615.1	0.0	0.0
Anheuser-Busch Inc. General Promotion	F310-8	541.8	541.8	0.0	0.0	0.0	0.0	0.0	0.0	0.0	0.0	0.0
Anheuser-Busch Lite Beer, Misc Brands	F310	9.7	0.0	0.0	0.0	9.7	0.0	0.0	0.0	0.0	0.0	0.0
Anheuser-Busch Products (Misc)	G619	13.8	13.8	0.0	0.0	0.0	0.0	0.0	0.0	0.0	0.0	0.0
Bud Dry Beer	F310	18,277.1	0.0	0.0	0.0	95.1	8,096.9	3,902.0	530.9	5,652.2	0.0	0.0
Bud Light Beer	F310	62,258.7	986.2	0.0	59.0	853.6	24,845.4	22,762.9	2,153.2	10,449.8	0.0	148.6
Bud Light Beer Concerts	F310	205.2	0.0	0.0	28.6	0.0	0.0	176.6	0.0	0.0	0.0	0.0
Bud Light Beer Sporting Events	F310	221.6	6.2	0.0	0.0	0.0	19.0	116.3	0.0	80.1	0.0	0.0
Budweiser Beer	F310	101,046.0	1,426.2	0.0	582.4	6,764.2	48,833.7	23,103.5	4,086.4	15,150.5	0.0	1,099.1
Budweiser Beer & Southwest Airline	F310	1.4	0.0	0.0	0.0	0.0	0.0	1.4	0.0	0.0	0.0	0.0
Budweiser Beer Concerts	F310	2,055.2	0.0	0.0	1,517.8	0.0	0.0	537.4	0.0	0.0	0.0	0.0
Budweiser Beer Sporting Events	F310	690.9	29.0	0.0	210.9	0.0	0.0	445.4	0.0	5.6	0.0	0.0
Budweiser Beer Trade Shows	F310	55.6	0.0	0.0	55.6	0.0	0.0	0.0	0.0	0.0	0.0	0.0
Budweiser Beer TV Program	F310-8	112.4	112.4	0.0	0.0	0.0	0.0	0.0	0.0	0.0	0.0	0.0
Budweiser Beers	F310	9,222.9	29.0	0.0	0.0	5.2	8,257.0	523.1	59.4	349.2	0.0	0.0
Budweiser Ice Draft Beer	F310	5,002.5	0.0	0.0	0.0	56.4	0.0	4,946.1	0.0	0.0	0.0	0.0
Budweiser Regular & Light Beers	F310	0.4	0.0	0.0	0.0	0.0	0.0	0.4	0.0	0.0	0.0	0.0
Busch Beer	F310	5,831.1	0.0	0.0	0.0	309.0	2,593.7	1,330.3	0.0	1,598.1	0.0	0.0
Busch Beer & Busch Light Beer	F310	12,632.7	0.0	0.0	0.0	0.0	6,306.6	3,038.5	0.0	3,287.6	0.0	0.0
Busch Gardens & Sea World Park	G322	106.3	0.0	0.0	0.0	0.0	0.0	106.3	0.0	0.0	0.0	0.0
Busch Gardens & St. Petersburg Clearwater	G322	149.9	0.0	0.0	0.0	0.0	0.0	149.9	0.0	0.0	0.0	0.0
Busch Gardens & Water Country USA	G322	176.6	0.0	0.0	0.0	30.8	0.0	145.8	0.0	0.0	0.0	0.0
Busch Gardens Amusement Park	G322	4,385.9	0.0	0.0	61.2	66.4	367.9	3,844.6	5.0	39.9	0.0	0.9
Busch Gardens Amusement Park Recruitment	B720-8	2.9	0.0	0.0	0.0	0.0	0.0	0.0	0.0	0.0	0.0	2.9
Busch Light Beer	F310	434.0	0.0	0.0	0.0	12.4	0.0	421.6	0.0	0.0	0.0	0.0
Parent Company Total		311,858.3	9,261.2	2.1	3,147.2	11,112.7	127,795.8	102,802.4	6,975.8	43,150.7	0.0	7,610.4

Source: Competitive Marketing Reporting.

the prime-time audience, today only about half of all viewers tune in to ABC, CBS, or NBC at that time, with the remainder watching cable networks or independent stations.

Share of Requirements

One of the most useful pieces of information you can examine is the source of your brand's sales. This is known as the *share of requirements*. It is calculated by taking the percentage of total category volume accounted for by a particular brand's users. Quite simply, it tells you whether your brand is being bought primarily by your customers or by your various competitors' customers. And, conversely, how much of your competitors' sales are coming from your brand users. Looking at this figure, you will be able to determine what percentage of the volume that you sell is accounted for by your users, as opposed to people who usually buy another brand.

Let's say you are a manufacturer of a local brand of pretzels (Pioneer Pretzels), competing with other regional brands as well as a major national brand. As you can see in the table below, Pioneer Pretzels buyers account for 27 percent of all the pretzels sold in the last 30 days. Of all the pretzels they purchase, 15 percent of their usage is to your brand (Pioneer), and 12 percent is to other brands. This means that 55 percent of their total category volume is given to your brand, which gives Pioneer a 55 percent share of requirements. This is the lowest figure among all pretzel types, suggesting that Pioneer's users are not especially brand loyal, which could harm sales and future market share.

	Total Category Volume	Brand Share of Volume	Brand Share of Requirements
National Pretzels	38%	25%	65%
Regional Pretzels	42	29	69
Pioneer Pretzels	27	15	55
Other Brands	9	5	65

Where Is Your Brand Sold?

Once you have found out as much as possible about how your brand stacks up against the competition, you need to think about geographic and distribution considerations. Specifically, you must look at where your brand is selling well and where it is doing poorly both in terms of regions, states, or markets, and in terms of type of retail outlet. This holds true whether your brand is available on a national, regional, or local basis. For unless your product is sold in just one store or location, there are likely to be some differences in sales according to geography and distribution outlet. What you discover by looking at the sales for your brand in these ways may lead you to develop a media plan with regional or local differences.

Indeed, today, more and more marketers are adopting a regional approach to selling, realizing that people in Boise have different tastes, customs, and buying habits than people in Boston or Baton Rouge. So marketers are customizing their marketing and media plans (and, in some cases, their products) to meet the needs of specific areas of the country. While some regional differences are obvious, such as higher snowblower sales in Maine than in Arizona, others might seem surprising (such as the fact that insecticides sell most heavily in the south). These types of differences occur not just at the product category level but also for individual brands. So Dannon yogurt sells far better on the East coast than does Yoplait, which has traditionally been stronger out West.

To understand geographic skews, the media specialist can turn to two pieces of information:

- Development indices.
- Market share.

Development Indices

You could, in theory, obtain sales data from every region or store in the country and look through them to find out your brand's sales picture. But a more efficient method for analyzing geographic strengths and weaknesses is to look at how the product category is doing across the U.S. and, then, how the brand is developing over time. Both of these are calculated by using *development indices.*

- **Category Development Index.** The category development index, or CDI, looks at product category sales in each potential region or market. A norm, or average, is calculated at 100, and then each area is assigned a value relative to that, expressed as a percent. Numbers below 100 indicate the category has lower than average sales in a given region, whereas those above 100 suggest sales of the category are greater than the national average in a certain part of the country.

So if, on average, 30,000 tractors are sold per month per region across the United States, that might mean 25,000 units are sold in the East, 45,000 in the West, and 33,000 in the South. So eastern sales would index at 83 (25,000/30,000), meaning that sales in that area are 17 percent below the national norm, while sales in the West would have a CDI of 150 (45,000/30,000), indicating that that region's sales are 50 percent higher than average. Those in the South have a CDI of 110 (33,000/30,000), which shows that southern sales are 10 percent higher than the norm. Based on such information, a company might decide to concentrate its marketing and media efforts in those regions with higher CDIs, as that is where there is greater potential for all tractor sales.

■ **Brand Development Index.** You should not rely solely on the CDI in making geographic media decisions, however. You also need to look at how your brand stacks up against other brands in the category. One tool for this job is the brand development index, of BDI. The calculation is very similar to that of the CDI. You calculate a norm, or average for all brands (or chief competitors) in the category, which is again set at 100, and then see how your own brand is doing in comparison. The John Deere tractor company might find its BDI for tractor sales is 10 percent above average in the eastern region and 5 percent below the norm in the West, suggesting that it is doing better than other brands in the category in the East, but slightly less well in comparison in the West.

When you look at the BDI, you need to keep the CDI in mind too. Once you have these two sets of data, you should compare your

EXHIBIT 2.6   BDI versus CDI

		Category Index	
		High	Low
Brand Index	High	Both brand and category growing	Brand growing and category declining
	Low	Brand declining and category growing	Both brand and category declining

BDI to your CDI. In that way you will be able to find those markets where your brand is doing better than the category overall and, conversely, where your brand appears to be underperforming the category (see Exhibit 2.6). For John Deere, its eastern BDI is greater than the CDI, so the brand is doing better than the category in that region. In the West, however, its BDI is below the CDI, so there is room for improvement here.

Armed with this information, you may choose to adopt one of three possible marketing and media strategies. You can focus your attention on those areas of the country where your brand is doing better than the category, playing to your strengths. Or you might choose to give more attention (and money) to the weaker markets where the category is doing well but your brand isn't, to try and bolster your sales there. Alternatively, you might decide to play it safe and concentrate on markets where both category and brand are successful. The one strategy you should probably avoid is pouring money into areas where both brand and category are doing poorly, as that suggests there is something about all the brands that is not liked or does not meet the needs of those consumers. To try and rectify that situation single-handedly is probably going to be more trouble (and cost) than it is worth.

Market Share

When looking at the development indices you can also find out how your competition is doing in each territory and even calculate their BDIs. It is common to see that where your brand is doing well, your competitors are having a harder time, and vice versa. The exception here would be for a new or relaunched category where all brands sell well, such as flavored mineral water.

One way of investigating sales further in geographic terms is to look at your share of the market by region or locality. Is your brand number one in sales in the Central region but in third place in the South? Are you neck-and-neck in New York, but a distant second in Florida? Faced with these different scenarios you probably want to explore some of the possible reasons behind the distinctions. And here you should go back to the other "Ps" of the marketing process. Perhaps you have *distribution* problems in Florida that are harming sales. Maybe your brand is being undercut in price in the South by a local manufacturer. Or it could be that your chief competitor is flooding the local airwaves with *promotional messages* in New York and drowning out yours. By putting together the information you gather from the development indices with your market share figures, you will start to create a picture of how your brand is doing across the country. That will help you decide what marketing and media tactics might be needed in each situation.

The media plan will not be the miracle solution to all of the problems you might encounter, and you should not expect it to turn a floundering brand into a superstar. But, as we shall see in subsequent chapters, the better your understanding of the marketing situation your brand is in, the more likely you are to come up with creative solutions to the problems. For example, if your problem is distribution, you might want to include extra trade promotions or incentives in your plan to encourage retailers or distributors to push your brand further. Pricing discrepancies might be alleviated by offering a coupon or on-pack premium to offset the lower-priced competitors. And if your consumers are being faced with a barrage of competitive messages in one medium, it might be wise to consider placing your own advertising in completely different media, or perhaps move to non-traditional media or special events to raise your own voice elsewhere.

Finally, if possible, you should try and look at your brand's geographic strengths and weaknesses over time to see where the trends are going. Have you always been weaker in the Southwest, or does this seem to have started only in the past year? Is the overall category development index flattening out across the country, or moving to different areas? This is especially likely to be true for new product categories when they are first introduced, as was the case for compact discs or dry beer. As always, looking at several years of data will help you to avoid acting on "blips" in the numbers that might have disappeared without cause within a few months.

A Word About Budgets

One of the most important preplanning issues to look at is how much money you are likely to have to spend for media for the coming year. You may be given a specific amount upfront, or you may have a range within which to work. In many situations, the media specialist is likely to come up with two or three alternative media plans at different spending levels, showing what could be achieved with $50,000, versus $75,000, versus $100,000, for example. We will say more about this in Chapter 7. If possible, you should try to be flexible on the budget at this point, keeping in mind that if you lock yourself into a set figure from the very beginning you may limit your creativity later on when you put the plan together.

Timing and Other Issues

The last major area to explore in the preplanning phase is that of timing. This may include the month of the year, the week of the month, the day of the week, or the hour of the day. While some timing considerations can be rationalized and justified, others may be out of your control. Some companies skew their messages towards pay periods, such as the 15th and 30th of the month, knowing that people are more likely to spend money when they have just been paid. Packaged-goods marketers may choose an end-of-week schedule to reflect the increase in grocery store shopping from Wednesday through Friday. Other considerations may be out of your control. The CEO of the company that makes your brand of sports drink may demand that you purchase television time during the Wimbledon tennis tournament because he likes tennis, or she may refuse to have the brand advertised in any magazine that accepts cigarette advertisements. Perhaps your light fixture company has been a sponsor of a local parade for the past fifty years and you cannot break with that tradition.

There might also be key timing opportunities that you should consider. If you are going into an Olympics year, you might want to look for some way to tie into that. While this sounds out of the league of any but the largest national advertisers, there may be an Olympic swim team member in your own town whom your brand of swim goggles could support in some way. Perhaps your city is celebrating its 200th anniversary and your pen factory has been around for almost as long, so you could get involved in the preparations for related events. Or maybe next year has been designated the Year of the Child so you can look for opportunities to promote your diaper brand. Be alert and open to new ideas and opportunities such as these that might come along infrequently and sporadically but could greatly enhance your profile and sales locally, regionally, or even nationally.

Summary

Before getting down to this year's plan it is important to know as much as possible about what has happened in the past. Find out as much as possible about how your company has operated in previous years, how your brand has performed, and what the competitors have done. Looking at trends in the product category is not only helpful, but might lead to new ways to define or position what you have to sell. Be aware of cultural, social, and economic forces that might impact your performance. As you examine your brand, consider who its real competitors are and learn about their past and present marketing plans. Determine your brand's share of market and share of requirements, too.

Pre-planning should also include an analysis of geographic variations in sales through category and brand development indices. Think about how consumers purchase and use your brand, how aware they are of it and its advertising, and when and how much they actually buy. Finally, keep in mind any budgeting or timing constraints that will affect your media plan.

Checklist—Media in the Marketing Context

1. Have you considered all elements of the marketing mix (price, place, product, and promotions)?
2. How much do consumers know about your brand?
3. Do you need to conduct research on your consumer, through focus groups, surveys, or analysis of syndicated data?
4. When do consumers buy your product? Which time of year, month, day of week or time of day?
5. How much do consumers buy? Is there a difference by product size or flavor?
6. Have you analyzed the history of your brand (how long it has been available, how successful it has been in the past, how it has been positioned in the past)? Include the company's history here, too.
7. What are your brand's chief competitors doing?
8. What are the product category trends?
9. How is your brand faring compared to competitors in terms of market share and share of requirements?
10. How does each major competitor position its brand and promote it?

11. Have you calculated the category and brand development indices for your brand?

12. Are there regional differences for your brand's sales and market share?

13. Have you considered any timing issues for the brand?

CHAPTER THREE

Developing Optimal Media Objectives

S etting objectives is something we are all familiar with in our day-to-day lives. "I will get an 'A' on this test;" "I'll lose 10 pounds by Christmas;" "My goal is to become the CEO of the company by the time I reach 35." Whatever the objective may be, if you didn't have one it would be difficult to know what you've achieved!

In the media planning context, you need to establish firm objectives for your plan in order to demonstrate how it will help your brand achieve its marketing goals. Although you may feel that in order to execute a media plan you must keep returning to your starting point, moving one step back for every two you go forward, it cannot be overemphasized that *everything* you do on the media planning side must be coordinated with the overall marketing strategy. Therefore, in order to establish your media objectives—what you intend the media plan to achieve—you must first reaffirm and clarify the goals of your complete advertising program to ensure that your media objectives fit in with the goals set in your brand's marketing objectives.

How the Marketing Objective Leads to the Media Objective

The media specialist is likely to be presented with the marketing objective rather than having to develop it on his or her own. It is usually stated in some quantifiable form, such as "sell x thousand more widgets in 1996 than in 1995," or "increase awareness of Brand X to 75 percent within calendar year 1995." It may relate to any of the major marketing functions, such as increasing shelf space in the store, or increasing the number of distribution channels for your product. And frequently it is expressed in terms of specific volume and share goals, such as "within calendar year 1995, bring Brand Z's total volume sold to 25 percent of the total category, raising its market share from 35 percent to 38 percent."

If the marketing objective is vague or ill-defined, simply "increasing awareness" or "improving distribution," then at the end of the year (or whatever time period has been set to achieve the goal) there is likely to be considerable debate over whether the plan was successful or not. It is also going to be more difficult for the media specialist to devise a plan that satisfies those objectives; even if awareness does improve, how much higher must it go in order for the media plan to be considered a success?

Along with understanding the marketing objective, the media specialist should also look at *how* that objective will be achieved, because that will affect what the media plan is supposed to do. Examples might be to increase product penetration among potential users by taking sales away from competitors or bringing new users into the marketplace. Alternatively, the strategy might be to encourage people to use your brand more frequently, perhaps offering new uses for it. So in order to increase the sales of Ragu Spaghetti Sauce, the marketing objective might be to get current users to buy additional jars of the product for use in new and different ways besides just pouring it onto spaghetti. For the media plan, this could lead to an objective of increasing the frequency with which target users are exposed to the message to remind them of the various ways they can use the product.

For a hospital with the marketing objective of introducing some new health education programs to encourage more people in the community to choose the facility for their medical needs, the media objective could be to reach 75 percent of those people living within ten miles of the location to inform them of everything the hospital can offer. Clearly, the marketing objective has a major impact on how the media plan develops, affecting the target audience, communications used, and media selected.

Media and the Advertising Objective

As we noted earlier, the marketing objective may relate to any of the four major areas of the marketing mix (product, promotion, distribution, or price). Therefore, before establishing specific media objectives it is also essential to focus on how the media affect your advertising goals. While your ultimate *marketing* goal for most goods is to sell more product (or services or image), unless your audience finds out about the product through the media that you use, that goal is unlikely to be reached. You need to be aware, at the same time, of the other marketing mix elements. If the product is no good, your media advertising will have little impact. Similarly, if you advertise your product heavily but it isn't available in most stores, sales will not improve.

Frequently, the objective of your advertising is tied in to the stage at which the target audience is in the decision-making process. As we noted earlier, this process breaks down into three very broad areas: Think, Feel, and Do (or, in research-speak, the *cognitive, affective,* and *conative* stages). Once you have decided that you need a new TV set you will *think* about what brands are available. Then, you will consider how you *feel* about each one of them. And finally, you will select a particular brand and take action (*do*) and buy it.

This process can be better understood by revisiting the eight main stages of the consumer decision-making process introduced in Chapter 2:

1. Need.
2. Awareness.

3. Preference.
4. Search.
5. Selection.
6. Purchase.
7. Use.
8. Satisfaction.

Need

Before you can hope to sell any more widgets, people have to have a reason to buy them. Contrary to what many advertising critics maintain, advertising cannot persuade people to buy something they do not want. Indeed, it is often easier to think of this first stage in the decision process as reflecting people's *wants,* for in today's industrial society most people are able to satisfy their basic needs, such as food and shelter.

Even when people buy products that seem pointless or silly, such as chia pets or hula hoops, they may feel they have a *need* to indulge in it just for fun. And while you might argue that no one really has a *need* for a $150,000 Rolls Royce, the person who chooses to purchase one clearly feels that he or she deserves this luxury automobile. Defining what the need might be for the product helps the marketer to understand the motivations behind why people might buy it, which in turn may provide some clues as to ways of reaching those people through the media. If you believe people are purchasing the business cards you print because they want to feel more confident in their business dealings, then to reach your target audience you could sponsor local seminars in winning new business.

Awareness

Once the consumer has determined that she needs a particular product, it is the job of marketing to make her aware of the choices that are available. For the media specialist, this means reaching that consumer in the right place and often enough so that your brand's message is the most relevant and convincing. And it is not enough to simply make people aware of your *brand*; the real goal here is to make them aware of your brand's *message*. For although you might well be able to reach 95 percent of all building contractors to make them aware of the roofing tile that you sell, unless they also learn that your tiles are 5 millimeters thicker than all others (and hence sturdier and more durable), your advertising is unlikely to increase sales. Of course, keep in mind that while you are promoting *your* message, every other tile company is also trying to boost awareness of its own brand.

Preference

Based on the various choices the consumer sees and hears, he or she will then develop specific brand preferences. Ideally, the marketer would like that consumer to develop *brand loyalty* to his brand so that every time Joe Smith needs to buy more glue, for example, he always picks up a bottle of Elmer's. A media plan to enhance preference might include opportunities for the target audience to try your brand at home, perhaps by offering a free sample.

Search

Once the target audience decides it might prefer your brand over others, the audience's next task is to find out where to purchase the item. Here, media advertising can be a big help, by notifying people of the places that sell your product. You have probably seen or heard this yourself in local or regional TV and radio ads that list which stores in your area stock the item. Billboards can be used, too, to display the retailer's or dealer's name. If your audience cannot find the product when it wants to buy it, then not even the best advertising placed in the most appropriate media will increase sales.

Selection

Brand selection may seem like an easy stage for the consumer. If she has decided already that she prefers your brand of nail polish over others, and has learned that it is sold in Wal-Mart stores, then isn't it obvious that she will buy it? Not necessarily. Today's consumer is faced with so many different brands that, once in the store and standing in front of the shelf, she may decide to go with your competitor's offering, because it is on sale, or packaged more attractively, or comes in larger bottles. So the selection process is a crucial stage for the marketer and the media specialist to consider. From a media perspective, the nail-polish user may be encouraged by in-store vehicles such as in-pack premiums or point-of-purchase radio. Personal contacts can also be very important at this stage. Someone who has come into the store in order to buy a mid-range computer may be encouraged to select your more expensive model by being offered one year of free parts and service by the dealer.

Purchase and Use

Clearly, the ultimate goal of marketing and media plans is to persuade consumers to purchase the product. But if they buy it and never use it, then there is no reason for them to ever buy another one. No marketer can remain successful by continually targeting new product users. So, often, one marketing and media objective is that of encouraging consumers to *use* the brand. In media planning terms, this might involve increasing the message frequency so that users are reminded of the different ways in which the brand can be used.

Satisfaction

The final stage in the consumer decision process is really a feedback loop into the earlier ones. If people use your private mail delivery service but are dissatisfied with the rate of delivery or quality of the staff, then their dissatisfaction will likely mean they won't use your service again. What is worse, they may tell their friends about their bad experience and decrease your potential sales even further. So customer satisfaction is extremely important for future success. *Satisfaction* is generally not listed as the primary marketing or media objective of a plan, but should nonetheless be kept in mind when deciding where and when to place your advertising message. It is perhaps harder to achieve through the media, because it is ultimately up to the user to decide whether he or she is satisfied. But many advertisers promise "satisfaction guaranteed or your money back" as a way to reassure consumers that they will, indeed, be content if they buy your brand.

Advertising Objectives and the Consumer Decision Process

To see how advertising objectives might fit in with each stage of the consumer decision process, let's take an example. If your company is a Health Maintenance Organization (HMO) offering employees a plan for managed healthcare, you would probably not have to create a "need" for your service. It is very likely, however, that you would want to increase awareness of your company's plans. So your advertising objective might be to boost awareness of the HMO from a baseline measure of 40 percent to 70 percent among employees at the companies which offer your plan.

It could be that most people know about your company, but are still choosing your main competitor as their healthcare provider. Here, your advertising objective would be to improve *preference,* so that instead of two out of five employees selecting your HMO over the other one, three out of five do so. Setting advertising objectives for the subsequent stages in the decision process is somewhat less common, because it is believed that advertising has a less direct role to play here. But you still might want to encourage consumers to *use* your HMO, setting as your advertising objective to boost member visits to your facilities from an average of two times per year to four by encouraging preventative care.

Media and the Consumer Decision Process

The advertising media will also affect each of these stages in the consumer decision process. To continue with the HMO example, you might boost *awareness* of your company through widespread local TV and radio ads or outdoor billboards in the communities where you have offices. Consumer *preference* could be encouraged by sending direct mail to potential members offering them a free check-up at one of your sites. They could be helped in the *search* process by putting ads that provide maps to your office locations in local newspapers. *Selection* might be helped by having open houses for new members to visit the doctors' offices and meet the personnel. These special events could then be promoted in local media and perhaps receive additional publicity through press releases. Finally, to get current members to *use* the HMO more for preventative care, you might create a monthly newsletter that tells them about the numerous programs you have available.

Let's take another example. Say you are in the market for a new automobile. That puts you in the initial stages of *needing* a new car. You see some TV ads for various makes and models, increasing your awareness of what is available. Three of the cars that interest you are the Honda Accord, the Volkswagen Passat, and the Ford Taurus. You read several automotive magazines and pick up the *Consumer Reports* issue on new cars and decide that these models fit your needs. So you have developed a *preference* for these particular models out of the hundreds that are available. Your next step would be to visit some car dealerships to *search* out the cars themselves. Here, your interaction with the salespeople is likely to play a major role in influencing your decision. You will also probably talk to friends and colleagues to find out about their experiences with each car, and discover their opinions. Faced with all of the information you have gathered, you *select* the Volkswagen. You negotiate a deal and drive the car home; now you can *use* it, and based on your experiences, you will develop a degree of *satisfaction* with your new purchase. If you are happy with the car, you may well buy another Volkswagen the next time you are in the car market.

The media's role is important at several points in the process. Television advertising is frequently used to create or enhance *awareness,* informing people of the qualities of the brand and what it has to offer. Both TV and magazines can help develop consumer *preference.* Here, you might see ads that compare the Volkswagen Passat to other cars in the same class, or that cite the awards and rankings the car has received in automotive competitions. And as we noted above, personal contacts and opinion leaders may play a vital role at this stage. Retail or local ads on spot radio and television and outdoor billboards help reach consumers who are *searching* for your brand; sometimes you will see a brief message from the local dealership tagged on to the end of a commercial.

To encourage people to *select* your offering, the media may offer special discounts or added features, such as a 60,000 mile warranty or $1,000 cash back. Getting people to *use* the product is also important. While this is not an issue in the case of an automobile, it can be for other consumer products. Bisquick, for instance, uses print ads that feature recipes for foods made with the baking mix in order to encourage people to take the product off the shelf.

As with the marketing objective, the more measurable the advertising objective is, the easier it will be to determine whether it has been achieved. This can be done either through specific testing after the ads have run for a while, or by setting up some kind of market test and determining the effect of advertising on sales.

Establishing Media Objectives

Armed with clear and concise marketing and advertising objectives, you are now ready for the most important part of the media planning process—setting media objectives. As with the other goals, once you have a clearly defined course set for you, it becomes much easier to figure out how to get there. There are three main elements involved in the media objectives:

- Defining the target audience.
- Setting broad communication objectives.
- Considering creative requirements.

Defining the Target Audience

Although you haven't yet started to put a plan together, you are probably beginning to realize that much of the most important work needs to be done beforehand to establish the media objectives. Defining the target audience is one key step you must take in the objective-setting process, for only by knowing who you wish to reach through the media will you be able to put together a schedule that will convey your brand's message to the right people.

Ideally, the target audience for your media plan should be identical to the audience for the overall marketing plan. Since most of a brand's sales are typically generated by its current users, the target audience definition is likely to include some product usage qualification. A marketing plan that is intended to increase sales of shampoo-conditioner combinations might have as its target audience "women 25 to 54 who currently use shampoo-conditioners, with an annual household income of more than $50,000". Life stage can be a crucial factor too. A plan geared towards increasing awareness of your new camcorder might have as its target "adults 18 to 49 who have had a child in the past year".

Often, however, you will often find that the media target may be both more and less precise than the marketing target. This is largely because the media themselves have traditionally been bought and sold on the basis of fairly basic demographics, such as age, sex, income, education, or race. So, for example, while your brand of crackers may be aiming to sell 20,000 more packets this year by expanding its user base and capturing more sales from "young adult gourmet lovers who enjoy entertaining and eating out", when it comes to creating your media objectives, your target may be "adults 18 to 34 with college education and an annual household income of more than $30,000." This is a more precise definition in that it specifies a particular age category as well as particular income and education levels, but it does not take into account (at least definitionally) the lifestyle variables (like eating out, entertaining, and fine foods).

Some advertising agencies have developed ways of examining people on the basis of these lifestyle or "psychographic" characteristics. The syndicated data sources of audience information are generally more limited in this respect. And if you are dealing with a non-consumer target, such as retailers or dealers, you may find yourself without much syndicated information at all, relying more on your experience and judgment. You can assume, for example, that if you are trying to promote your refrigeration equipment to restaurants one place to put your message would be *Restaurant News*.

Another important consideration for defining your media target is whether it should be broad or narrow. Because everyone in the country uses laundry detergent, does that mean your media plan should be aimed at "all adults in the United States who use laundry detergent"? Increasingly, the answer will be "no." Today's brands are becoming more and more segmented. So we don't just have one box of Tide on the store shelf, but powder or liquid Tide, Tide with Bleach, or Ultra (concentrated) Tide. And the detergent comes in six different sizes to suit the needs of different people, from singles living alone to large families. Each of these groups is likely to have different media habits and preferences—and trying to create a media plan that would reach everyone would ignore the needs of different population groups both in terms of product benefits and media usage. There might be one plan aimed at mothers with young children, another for those with large families, another with an environmental slant, and a fourth promoting the liquid version. Each plan has a different target audience.

There is also the opposite danger, however. That is, you might define your target audience so narrowly that it would be almost impossible to reach them. You might, from previous research into who buys your desk organizers, find that they are most likely to be men with a median age of 39 who work as salesmen traveling in the northeast region of the country taking on average three business trips per month, earning $50,000 or more a year, with a non-working wife and three children, living in the suburbs, owning an American-made car, and enjoying computer games. But there may be only 50 of them!

There are two major problems to note here. First, most traditional media will not only present your message to *your* target, but also to many others for whom the product is probably irrelevant. This is a problem that can only be alleviated by careful consideration of exactly who your target should be and which media will best reach that audience.

A second consideration in establishing media objectives is the cost effectiveness of the plan. It may well be the chief concern of you or of the top executives of your company. You could come up with an extremely elaborate and highly targeted media plan, with a clearly defined target audience and appropriate communication objectives, but if it is going to cost twice as much as is in the marketing budget, you are unlikely to be able to execute it. So when defining the target audience, you must be sure that the audience will be reachable at an affordable cost. As the maker of Oral B toothbrushes you cannot hope to reach everyone who brushes their teeth on a budget of $10 million.

Having defined your target audience, your next step should be to find out as much as possible about the individuals who make up that audience. Ideally, you should not only know their basic demographic characteristics (age, sex, education level, income, profession, etc.), but also learn more about the kinds of products they use and the media they tend to hear or see. Again, depending on the target, you can often obtain this information from syndicated data services. Or you may have to rely on your own judgment and experience. So if your target for a portable computer is men 25 to 54 who take six or more plane trips per year, you should also know that they are also

EXHIBIT 3.1   Profile of Frequent Flyer Target

Men 25–54, *flying 6+ time per year are:*

more likely to	*less likely to*
read magazines on Business, Computers, Cities, News, Science, Sports, Travel	*read magazines on* Fishing, Mechanics
listen to Adult Contemporary, All News Classic Rock, Classical News/Talk	*listen to* Album-oriented rock (AOR) Country
watch Baseball Specials Basketball Specials News General Drama Primetime Golf or tennis	*watch* Adventures/westerns Comedy/variety Pageants Detective/suspense Situation comedies
Own Home Computer Drink imported beer Own American Express Gold Card	Own Truck Drink domestic beer

Source: Mediamark Research, Inc., 1993.

more likely to have a computer in their home, drink imported beer, own an American Express Gold Card, read business magazines, listen to All News radio stations, and watch golf or tennis on TV.

Communication Objectives

When it comes to writing down what you expect the advertising message to do for your brand, you will start to find that all of a sudden you are dealing with the art, rather than the science, of media planning. These objectives are measurable to some degree through communications tests with the target audience that find out what information the audience is taking away from the message. In addition, media calculations can be made to estimate what the plan should achieve. But many of the criteria you need to use to establish what the goals should be are far more evaluative and rely on your judgment and subjective response to everything that you know about the brand, its advertising, and the marketplace. These objectives must also be in line with the overall marketing strategy for the brand. If you are trying to increase your market share of the athletic shoe category by 2 percentage points by increasing distribution into mass merchandise outlets, then your communication objective might involve increasing awareness of your brand among your target audience by 15 percent within the first three months of the campaign.

Communication objectives will vary, depending upon the kind of product you are promoting. For a new brand of cat litter, you probably want your advertising to generate awareness of the product. If you are advertising Maytag dishwashers, in contrast, which have been around forever, your message will more likely serve as a reminder to consumers of the reliability of the product. These differing objectives will also affect your reach and frequency goals. For a new product, you would want to establish some initial awareness levels and then sustain them (for example, generate awareness of the product among 75 percent of the target group within the first three months of the campaign).

Don't forget to consider your competition, too. You might set as your objective to achieve, within the first six months of your new campaign, awareness levels for your brand of fountain pen that are equal to or greater than those of your closest competitor. Geography is another factor. If your fishing rod is the number-one brand in the category with the highest awareness levels in the northeast and southeast, but falls to number two or three in the West, then you might set different objectives in different parts of the country, adding more frequency in areas where awareness levels are currently lower.

There are three main factors to consider when developing communication objectives: campaign timing, category and brand dynamics, and media reach and frequency.

- **Campaign Timing.** Here you should consider what stage your campaign is at—are you launching a new product or changing the strategy for selling it, or is this the third or fourth year of an ongoing campaign? Also think about the specific timing of the campaign. Are you trying to communicate a seasonal message to warn young adults about drinking and driving during the holidays? Or maybe it's April and people are starting to think about preparing their swimming pools for summer, so it's the perfect time to begin promoting your pool cleaning service. Thinking of your communications objectives within a specific timeframe will help to ensure that your media plan stays focused on that period.

- **Category and Brand Dynamics.** If you study the trends for your brand in particular as well as trends within the category overall, your communication objectives will be firmly fixed in reality. That is, if research shows that users of lawn-care products are extremely brand loyal it makes little sense to say the objective for your brand of weed-killer is to gain 15 market-share points from your competitors in the next 12 months. Related to loyalty, you should think also about what degree of consumer involvement with the category can be reasonably expected. It's hard to get people excited about staplers or canned tomatoes, no matter how wonderful your creative message or media plan.

  Try to be objective about your brand's positioning, too. Is your advertising message really very different from competitors', or is it in fact just another version of the same idea? If you look at the advertising for most products, you'll see that the latter is far more common than the former. Almost all banks tout their low financing rates, while nearly all beers talk about great taste, and most garbage bags emphasize their strength. None of this should be too surprising; you wouldn't want to buy a beer that didn't taste good, or a garbage bag that wasn't strong.

- **Reach and Frequency.** Having stated earlier that communication objectives tend to be more subjective than objective, more art than science, there is still a role for some numbers here. But they should only be included if you will have some way of measuring them. The two key concepts to consider here are *reach* and *frequency*. These are the two most commonly used media terms in the whole planning process. The *reach* of the plan refers to the number (or percentage) of the target audience that will be reached by the brand's advertising in the media. As we shall learn in Chapter 5, that number is determined by calculating what percentage of the target audience will be exposed to the media in which your ad appears.

Along with knowing how many people will have the opportunity to see or hear your ad, you also need to state how many times they need to do so in order for the message to have some effect. This is the concept of *effective frequency.* You should identify some reach and frequency goals as a way of measuring whether your communication objectives were achieved. If the communication goal is to "increase awareness of the brand by 10 percent among the key consumer target," then that can be measured by establishing what percentage of the target was actually reached with the message and how many times they heard it, and whether brand awareness levels did in fact go up. More will be said on this topic in Chapter 5.

Creative Requirements

The last area that should be considered in preplanning discussions is any special creative requirement that will affect the media selected. If you are introducing a new car and want to emphasize its solid engineering through long copy and details, you will have to think in terms of the media that can allow you to do that. Or, if your task is to promote Chicago as a vacation destination for families, then the creative might consist of many different sights or sounds from that city to convey the desired image. The message will, in part, determine where you choose to place it. Yet another example might be introducing a new cake mix. Your ads will showcase the delicious results of using the product, so the visual element is going to be particularly important. Immediately, this leads you in a certain direction when starting to consider your media plan strategies and tactics.

Summary

In order for a media plan to be successful, it must be tied directly to the broad marketing objectives for the brand, usually defined in terms of sales and market share. The goals for media should also be derived from the advertising objectives, which show where the advertising fits in to the consumer's decision process, such as increasing awareness or improving customer satisfaction, or generating additional use of the product. The media objectives state to whom the message is to be delivered (the target audience), when it is to be distributed (timing specifics), and how many times a given proportion of the target will, ideally, be exposed (media reach and frequency). Special creative requirements for the brand's communications should also be taken into account.

Checklist—Developing Optimal Media Objectives

1. Do you know your brand's marketing objectives?
2. Are they stated clearly and explicitly, in an actionable way?
3. What is the advertising objective for the brand?
4. Have you considered where the advertising might fit in with the eight stages of the consumer decision process—need, awareness, preference, search, selection, purchase, use, and satisfaction?
5. In which stage of the consumer decision process does your advertising objective fit?
6. Have you clearly defined your target audience, or audiences?
7. What are your communication objectives, in terms of a specific timeframe, given the competitive situation?
8. What are your media reach and frequency goals?
9. Are there any specific creative requirements for the brand's message?

CHAPTER FOUR

Exploring
the Media

We are all familiar with television, radio, newspapers or magazines from the consumer's standpoint. That is, we don't think twice about picking up the newspaper every morning, listening to the radio on the way to work, watching TV when we get home at night, and leafing through a magazine in bed before going to sleep. For advertisers, each of those points of contact we make with the medium represents an opportunity to communicate with a potential target for their product or service. So, for example, the local car dealer will place his ad for a Ford Taurus in the daily newspaper in the hope that you will see it in the morning and stop in at the dealership on the way home from work or at the weekend. The First National Bank might put an ad on the radio in the morning hours to reach commuters on their way to work to alert them to the bank's favorable interest rates on savings accounts. When you sit back and relax in the evening to watch television, a wide range of advertisers will remind you of their brand of beer, soap, pet food, or coffee, hoping that when you next visit the grocery store theirs is the brand you will select. And finally, right before you fall asleep, advertisers in magazines will try to persuade you that their insurance company will be there when you need it.

Media Categories

Once you have clearly defined media objectives, the next step will be to decide which media types, and vehicles within those types, will best help you achieve your goals. Before exploring that further, we need to think about what the different media can offer you as an advertiser conveying an advertising message. Here, we will consider the five major media categories: television, radio, magazines, newspapers, and out-of-home. Keep in mind, though that there are many other alternatives available to you, such as direct mail, public relations, or promotions.

There are various ways of categorizing the media. We can contrast the *print* media of magazines, newspapers and outdoor billboards with *electronic* media—radio and TV. We can also make an important distinction between media that are predominantly *local* (newspapers, outdoor billboards, and radio) and those where most ads are placed on a *national* basis (TV and magazines). Here, we will look at the major characteristics of each media form.

A Television in Every Home

Almost every household in America has a television set, while two-thirds (64 percent) have two or more. Television is the largest mass medium available for advertisers. In 1993, $30 billion were spent promoting goods and services this way. People in the United States have their TV sets on, on average, 7 hours each day, which is one of the highest viewing figures of anywhere in the world.

Broadcast television programming is usually divided up in two ways: by *daypart* and by *format.* The daypart refers to the time of day the program airs. There are nine standard dayparts, which are shown in Exhibit 4.1.

EXHIBIT 4.1   Dayparts—Eastern Standard Time

Early Morning	Daytime	Early Fringe
M–F	M–F	M–F
7:00–9:00 A.M.	9:00 A.M.–4.30 P.M.	4:30–7:30P.M.
Prime Access	Primetime	Late News
M–F	M–S 8:00–11:00 P.M.	M–Sun.
7:30–8:00 P.M	& Sun. 7:00–11:00 P.M.	11:00–11:30 P.M.
Late Night	Saturday Morning	Weekend Afternoons
M–Sun.	Sat.	Sat.–Sun.
11:30–1:00 A.M.	8:00 A.M.–1:00 P.M.	1:00 P.M.–7:00 P.M.

Program formats are also standardized into 14 main types, which are given in Exhibit 4.2.

EXHIBIT 4.2   Formats

Animation/Children
Daytime Serials
Drama/Adventure
Games
Late Night Talk
Movies
News
Prime-Time News
Reality-Based
Sitcoms
Specials
Sports
Talk

Again, it is worth emphasizing that these breakdowns are really only the concern of the programmers and advertisers; you don't choose to watch "Situation Comedies" or "Video/Variety," but rather decide to watch "Wide World of Sports" on ABC on Sunday afternoon.

There are four main types of television to consider: network, syndication, spot (local) and cable. You, as the viewer, do not differentiate between them—you choose to watch a certain program, regardless of how or where it airs. So the distinctions we draw here are purely for media purposes.

Network Television

Network television consists of the four broadcast networks: ABC, CBS, NBC, and the relative newcomer, FOX. A "network" is actually made up of hundreds of local stations that become "affiliates" of the national organization. Each station receives a set amount of money every year from the network in return for which they agree to air national programs for a given number of hours every week. Network programs air at the same time in every market within a given time zone. So "60 Minutes" appears at 7 P.M. on Sunday night in the Eastern zone, 6 P.M. in Central markets, and 5 P.M. in the Mountain zone. Programs in the Pacific time zone are shown at the same time locally as in the East (i.e., "60 Minutes" airs at 7 P.M. Pacific time).

Network shows come with several minutes of commercial time both within and between programs that are sold by the network. The local station is then able to sell an additional one to three minutes of commercial time in the hour for breaks between programs to local or regional advertisers, depending on the daypart. The local station also decides what to air when it is not showing network programs. This might include locally produced shows, such as local news or current affairs programs, or programs purchased from independent producers, known as syndicated programming (see below).

Stations not affiliated with a network are known as *independents*. Today, there are more than 300 such stations in the United States. Each one decides which programs to air throughout the broadcast day, and is responsible for selling its own commercial time.

Syndication

One of the major sources of programs for independent stations is syndicated programming. Here, an individual program (or package of several programs) is sold on a station-by-station basis, regardless of that station's affiliation. It may be of any type or length. There are two main types—original shows, and off-network fare. The former tend to be primarily game shows, such as *Wheel of Fortune*, and talk shows such as *Oprah*. They are sold either by the program's producers or by syndication companies such as King World which puts together packages of properties. The distinction between syndication and network shows is that syndicated programs can air at different times in different markets as well as on different networks. This leads to syndicated shows having to be "cleared" by each local station that chooses to buy them. The clearance figure refers to the percentage of markets across the country that are able to view that particular show. So, for example, if a syndicated talk show is "cleared" in 70 percent of the United States, it means that broadcast TV stations seen by 70 percent of all TV viewers have purchased that program. Syndication clearances generally range anywhere from 70 percent to 99 percent. It is worth noting, too, that some network programs do not have total (100 percent) clearance because an affiliate station may refuse to air them, or will put them on at a different time than the rest of the network. A recent example of this is the controversial police drama on ABC, "NYPD Blue," which, even though it received good ratings and won numerous awards, could still not be seen by viewers of the ABC affiliates in several Texas markets because they felt the program was too offensive.

EXHIBIT 4.3　Top Ten Syndicated Programs

Top Ten Shows in Syndication: September 1992–April 1993		
Rank	Program	Household Rating (%)
1.	Wheel of Fortune	14.1
2.	Jeopardy	12.3
3.	Star Trek: The Next Generation	12.2
4.	Star Trek: Deep Space Nine	10.9
5.	Oprah Winfrey Show	10.4
6.	Entertainment Tonight	8.8
7.	Magic II	8.2
8.	Married . . . with Children	7.9
9.	Wheel of Fortune—Weekend	7.8
10.	Current Affair	7.5

Source: Nielsen Media Research, Report on Television 1992–93.

Spot Television

Spot television is the another way to purchase television time. Here, instead of contracting with the network to distribute a commercial to all of that network's affiliate stations across the country, an advertiser can pick and choose which programs and stations to use, placing the message in various "spots" across the country. The buy could be as small as a single station in one market, to a couple of hundred stations across a region. While the actual cost of placing spots on local stations is lower than a total network buy, once you start including a large number of markets it can become quite expensive.

Spot TV time is sold either by the individual station and/or by station representative firms, or *rep firms*. These firms put together packages of stations, known as *unwired networks* (because they are not physically linked together, or wired). Rep firms can usually customize buys for you, allowing you to pick only those stations that you are interested in in a given number of markets.

Cable Television

Cable television is often thought of as a relatively new way to distribute programs and commercials, but in fact it has existed as a means of conveying television signals since 1948. Because it does not depend on over-the-air signals, but comes into the home via wires laid underground (or sometimes on poles on the street), reception is much clearer in many areas. That was the original reason behind its growth—so that people in Eugene, Oregon, or Lancaster, Pennsylvania could receive the signals of the broadcast networks more clearly. While the broadcast networks distribute their programs from a central location to each of their affiliates, cable programs are sent via satellite from the cable network to individual cable operators (franchises) within each market, who then distribute the signals to the subscribers' homes. There are more than 10,000 separate cable systems operating today, although the majority belong to one of the large Multiple System Operators (MSOs) that have cable systems in numerous markets.

Another difference between broadcast TV and cable TV, from the consumers' standpoint, is that they must pay a monthly subscription fee to receive cable service. The average monthly cost of cable in 1993 was $23. For an additional monthly fee, consumers can receive one or more of the pay cable networks, such as Home Box Office (HBO), Showtime, or The Disney Channel, which do not show any advertising at all.

Cable TV is made up of a wide variety of different networks, many of which specialize in certain kinds of programs or appeal to certain types of people. This was originally called *narrowcasting*, in contrast to the more diverse or broad-based programming found on broadcast TV. Cable News Network (CNN) shows 24 hours of news and information programming, while ESPN airs sports all the time and Comedy Central has 24 hours of comedy. There are several cable networks, such as USA Network and The Family Channel, which are more similar to the broadcast networks in their programming, airing a variety of different types of shows, from adventures to situation comedies to movies and dramas. Exhibit 4.4 describes the biggest cable networks currently available, together with the number of subscribers to each one.

EXHIBIT 4.4 Cable Networks and Subscribers

Network	Subscribers (000)
American Movie Classics	44,542
Arts & Entertainment Network	57,114
Black Entertainment Television	39,579
Bravo	12,650
CNBC	50,632
Cable News Network (CNN)	61,614
The Cartoon Network	10,197
C-SPAN	59,800
C-SPAN II	29,700
Comedy Central	30,296
Country Music Television	24,895
Courtroom Television Network	14,435
The Discovery Channel	60,486
E! Entertainment Television	26,034
ESPN	61,804
ESPN2	12,600
The Family Channel	57,874
Headline News	53,164
Home Shopping Network	21,000
The Learning Channel	28,297
Lifetime	58,588
MTV	59,457
The Nashville Network	58,123

(continued)

EXHIBIT 4.4   Cable Networks and Subscribers *(continued)*

Network	Subscribers (000)
Nickelodeon	60,929
Nick at Nite	51,250
QVC Network	46,300
The Sci-Fi Channel	15,579
TBS Superstation	60,504
Telemundo	13,320
TNT	59,975
The Travel Channel	20,074
Univision	11,062
USA Network	61,193
VH-1	49,573
The Weather Channel	55,443
Pay Cable	
Cinemax	6,900
The Disney Channel	7,730
Home Box Office	17,900
The Movie Channel	2,700
Showtime	7,600

Source: *Cablevision Magazine,* June 13, 1994.

The number of networks available varies by system. Those that were built in the 1950s and 1960s typically have smaller channel capacities than do newer systems. Today, some franchises operate systems with 150 channels on them. And there are plans to set up systems with up to 500 different channels! Such large capacity will become increasingly common as the technology improves to allow for it. Exhibit 4.5 shows how the number of stations and channels available to viewers has increased over the past 15 years.

The development of cable TV as an advertising medium began in the early 1980s and has grown steadily ever since. Today, $2 billion of total TV advertising dollars go to cable television, representing 6 percent of the total amount advertisers spend in television. Most of cable's ad dollars are purchased on a national basis, although the medium has been growing rapidly at the local level, too. If you manage a local restaurant or a bank, you can run your commercials throughout the area, or can confine your messages to a particular

EXHIBIT 4.5   System Channel Capacity

Number of Channels and Stations Received

Percent of Households that Can Receive Broadcast Over-the-Air Stations

	1–6	7–10	11–14	15+	Average
1981	25%	32%	36%	7%	9.1%
1985	13	40	25	22	11.0
1993	5	24	35	35	13.3

Percent of Households that Can Receive Channels (Over-the-Air Stations + Cable)

	1–6	7–10	11–14	15+	Average
1981	25%	22%	40%	13%	NA
1985	8	17	25	50	18.8
1993	4	9	7	80	39.4

Source: Nielsen Media Research Report on Television 1992–93.

cable system's area. National advertisers can also use local cable, customizing their messages down to the neighborhood (system) level.

You can purchase time on several systems at once by going through a central sales office, known as an *interconnect*. This is similar to a rep firm—you select the cable systems on which your ad will appear. Most interconnects operate on a metropolitan or regional basis, such as Greater Chicago, or the Bay Area.

New Forms of Television

In the early 1990s several important developments were announced or introduced in the world of television that will eventually hold important implications for advertisers. One of the most firmly established, at this point, is *pay-per-view* (PPV). Here, several channels are allocated to special programs, such as movies or sporting events, that are purchased by the cable subscriber on an individual basis. They may cost as little as a few dollars, or as much as $35 for a special boxing match, for example. In order to be able to receive this form of programming, the cable linking the television to the cable system operator must be two-way, or *addressable,* allowing the operator to deliver the program to individual households on demand. In the future, we are likely to see more and more of this form of "video on demand," particularly in a world in which the viewer controls exactly what she wishes to see.

That world is not so far away anymore. The two largest cable system operators—Tele-Communications, Inc. (TCI) and Time Warner are each working on developing sophisticated multi-channel systems. Many of those channels will carry movies or special events that the viewer will pay for on an individualized basis. He may also be able to choose individual programs and view them whenever he wants rather than when the network has scheduled them. Other possibilities include long-form commercials, or infomercials, that the viewer can call up when interested in buying a car or taking a vacation, for example. Home shopping is predicted to be a major opportunity for advertisers in the television of tomorrow, allowing people to select individualized styles, colors, and sizes, see them modeled on the screen, and then purchase them by credit card simply by pushing a button on their remote control. Ultimately, instead of TV being a form of mass communication, the medium will become a means of one-to-one, or personalized electronic marketing.

Benefits of Television to Advertisers

Whichever type of television advertising you choose, you will enjoy a number of benefits unavailable from any other media. Among these benefits, television's ability to imitate real-life situations, its pervasiveness, and its broad reach are especially remarkable.

True to Life

The most obvious advantage of television advertising is the opportunity to use *sight, sound, color,* and *motion* in commercials. This form of advertising is generally considered the most lifelike, re-creating scenes and showing people in situations with which we can all identify. That does not mean we don't see cartoons or animated commercials, or fantasies on the screen; today's electronic wizardry lets TV ads show us everything imaginable. But of all the media available, TV comes closest to showing us products in our everyday lives. This is not only important for package goods advertisers—firms such as Pillsbury, Anheuser-Busch, or Dial, who are able to show us what their products look like and how they are used or enjoyed—but also for service companies such as Marriott Hotels or American Express, which can offer us ways to use their amenities.

The Most Pervasive Medium

Television advertising is the most pervasive media form available. Several slogans from TV commercials have entered the mainstream of conversation, such as the famous "Where's the beef?" used in ads for Wendy's hamburgers, or Wisk detergent's infamous "ring around the collar" line. Characters in commercials have also become part of our lives, such as the lonely Maytag repairman, or Tony the Tiger for Kellogg's Frosted Flakes.

Reaching the Masses

Another important advantage of television from an advertising perspective is the wide *reach* of people it offers at any one time. Even in programs with ratings of 8 or 10 (see Exhibit 4.3), you are reaching about 9 million individuals! While there is generally a smaller audience for the commercials than for the programs themselves, nevertheless, television remains a truly mass medium. Moreover, by buying time on several different programs shown at different times and/or on different days, it is possible to reach a wide *variety* of individuals. And although an individual ad appears for a short time (usually 15 or 30 seconds), if it is repeated on several occasions more people are likely to be exposed to it, often more than once. This helps build brand awareness, which in turn may lead to the formation of favorable attitudes or intentions to purchase that brand.

Drawbacks of Television Advertising

Unfortunately, television advertising has unique drawbacks as well as the unique benefits we've just discussed. Four of the most commonly encountered drawbacks are cost, limited exposure time, cluttered airwaves, and poor placement of ads within or between programs.

Dollars and Sense

Perhaps the biggest disadvantage for advertising on TV, particularly at the national level, is the high cost. The average 30-second commercial during prime time in 1993 cost $200,000. An ad in the 1995 Superbowl, television's most expensive ad opportunity, cost up to

EXHIBIT 4.6   TV Commercial Costs: Prime Time 1994–95 Season

Program	Cost per:30	Network	Program Type
Seinfeld	$390,000	NBC	Sitcom
Home Improvement	$350,000	ABC	Sitcom
Roseanne	$310,000	ABC	Sitcom
Murphy Brown	$290,000	CBS	Sitcom
NFL Monday Night Football	$285,000	ABC	Sports
Frasier	$230,000	NBC	Sitcom
Northern Exposure	$225,000	CBS	Drama
Ellen	$225,000	ABC	Sitcom
60 Minutes	$225,000	CBS	News/Reality
Mad About You	$220,000	NBC	Sitcom
The Simpsons	$210,000	FOX	Sitcom
NYPD Blue	$180,000	ABC	Drama
Coach	$175,000	ABC	Sitcom
Dr. Quinn: Medicine Woman	$175,000	ABC	Drama
Married . . . with Children	$175,000	FOX	Sitcom
Melrose Place	$150,000	FOX	Drama
Beverly Hills, 90210	$150,000	FOX	Drama
20/20	$150,000	ABC	News/Reality
Rescue: 911	$145,000	CBS	News/Reality
Murder, She Wrote	$145,000	CBS	Drama
48 Hours	$140,000	CBS	News/Reality
SeaQuest DSV	$130,000	NBC	Drama
NBC Monday Night Movie	$125,000	NBC	Movie
Full House	$125,000	ABC	Sitcom
The X-Files	$115,000	FOX	Drama
Dateline NBC	$105,000	NBC	News/Reality
Cops	$95,000	FOX	News/Reality

Source: Advertising Age, October 1994.

$1,000,000. For many advertisers this is way beyond their budget, leading them to cable or spot TV as cheaper alternatives.

Quick Cuts

Another drawback to this medium is its brief exposure time. Although many ads are seen several times within a short period of time, unless the commercial is particularly inventive or unusual it is likely the viewer will ignore it or be irritated by seeing it after the first few occasions. Controversy remains over just how many times people can be exposed to spots without getting bored or annoyed, a phenomenon referred to as commercial *wearout*. In the future, this drawback may be avoided through *infomercials,* or long-form commercials lasting from five to thirty minutes or longer that present information on a specific brand or product in detail. The key here is that this self-selected audience is more interested and involved in the message.

Cluttering the Airwaves

A related factor that is becoming an increasing concern for advertisers is the sheer number of ads appearing on TV. This leads to clutter of spots, again believed to reduce the effectiveness of individual commercials. There is evidence to support this fear. From 1982 to 1992 there was a 26 percent increase in the number of spots shown on prime-time network TV. Part of the explanation for this is the increase in the number of shorter-length commercials. For many years, the standard television spot lasted a full minute. Then, in the mid-1960s more and more advertisers started using 30-second commercials, finding them more cost-efficient and no less effective. As costs continued to increase during the 1970s and early 1980s, advertisers tried the same

EXHIBIT 4.7 Growth of 15-Second Commercials

	:60	:30	:15	Other
1975	5%	95%	0%	0%
1980	2	96	0	2
1985	3	84	11	2
1990	2	61	35	2
1992	2	63	32	3

Source: DDB Needham Worldwide Media Trends 1994; data supplied by Competitive Media Reporting.

tactic, shifting to even smaller commercial lengths. Today, the 15-second spot accounts for 38 percent of all network TV commercials.

Placing Spots

Another area that has provoked a good deal of discussion is where commercials should be placed for optimal effectiveness. For network TV, you can buy time either within the program (*in-program*) or between two shows (*break*). While some believe there is no difference in viewer attention between these two options, others feel that you are likely to lose more viewers during the breaks than within the program itself. On spot TV there is no choice; only the break position is available.

Related to this placement issue is where to position your commercial within the series, or *pod* of spots being shown. Evidence suggests that the first ad to appear will receive the most attention, followed by the last one; those in the middle are likely to suffer from viewers switching channels, not looking at the screen, or leaving the room. The advertiser, however, does not get the choice of where in the pod to air his ad.

Radio—The "Everywhere" Medium

Radio is the oldest electronic advertising medium. It first became popular in America in the early 1920s and since that time has managed to hold its own against all other media forms. Although families no longer sit around their radios as they once did to listen to the most popular programs of the day, they still rely on this medium for both information and entertainment. Indeed, almost every home in America has at least one radio, and most have several of them. People listen to the radio, on average, for 3 hours 17 minutes every day. Most listening (84 percent) occurs between 6 A.M. and 10 A.M. Increasingly, that listening occurs outside of the home. Almost all cars (95 percent) are fitted with radios now, and people can carry the medium with them wherever they go.

There are more than 10,000 radio stations across the country. Of those, 4,990 operate on the AM (Amplitude Modulation) wavelength, while 5,873 are FM, or Frequency Modulation, stations. The primary differences between them are in reception area and audience. AM stations can broadcast over a wider distance, but as a result, the sound quality is inferior to the more restricted FM stations. AM tends to be listened to more by older adults, reflecting the fact that more AM stations offer news and talk programs rather than the music formats which dominate the FM wavelength. Radio stations are either commercial, accepting advertising as their chief source of revenue, or non-commercial, funded by public monies and/or audience sponsorships. Commercial stations, on average, will air between 9 and 12 ads per hour, frequently concentrated at the top and bottom of the hour.

As with television, radio is classified by both daypart and format. The different formats that are available for the advertiser are not defined the same way by the listener. Radio dayparts and formats are shown in Exhibits 4.8 and 4.9, below.

EXHIBIT 4.8   Radio Dayparts

Morning Drive	6:00 A.M.–10:00 A.M.
Daytime	10:00 A.M.–3:00 P.M.
Afternoon Drive	3:00 P.M.–7:00 P.M.
Evening	7:00 P.M.–Midnight
Late Night	Midnight–6:00 A.M.

EXHIBIT 4.9   Radio Formats

Adult Contemporary/Soft Rock	Country
Contemporary Hit Radio (CHR)	Album Oriented Rock (AOR)/Classic Rock
Oldies	Middle-of-the-Road (MOR)/Nostalgia
All News/News Talk	Religious
Spanish	Easy Listening
Urban Contemporary	Black
Talk	New Age/Jazz
Gospel	Classical
Ethnic	

Today, radio represents 7 percent of all advertising expenditures. The two main types of radio advertising are network (national) and spot (local). The way programs and ads are distributed is similar to that of network and spot broadcast TV.

Network Radio

Unlike television, network radio is less important than local radio is to advertisers. It currently receives 5.5 percent of all radio dollars. Like TV, however, a message placed on network radio is distributed via satellite to each network's affiliate stations. These stations are paid an annual sum to take, or "clear," the network's programs. Perhaps surprisingly, almost two-thirds of all radio stations are affiliated with one network or another. The kinds of programs they receive from the network may be aired every day, such as the ABC newscast, or periodically, such as *Casey Kasem's Weekly Top 40* show. There are presently four major radio networks, each of which has subdivisions based on the programming and the demographic make-up of their listeners. So ABC Excel is aimed primarily at listeners from 18 to 34 years old, while the stations that are part of ABC Galaxy tend to be favored by adults over age 35. Exhibit 4.10 lists the major networks.

EXHIBIT 4.10   Radio Networks

ABC
CBS
Westwood One
American Urban Radio Network (AURN)

From an advertiser's perspective, one key benefit of using network radio is that you can go through a single source to place your ads across a region or across the country. The downside of this form of radio, however, is that you have less flexibility in choosing the stations you wish to be in. If you buy the CBS Spectrum Radio Network, you may get the Number 1 station in Biloxi, Mississippi, but a distant fourth station in Little Rock, Arkansas.

Spot Radio

Nearly 95 percent of radio's advertising dollars are spent in spot markets, where you buy time on individual stations on a market-by-market basis. Here, if you were advertising your chain of realtors, you could buy time on individual stations in a market, regardless of which network they belong to, and choose which markets you wished to target. The advantage of purchasing radio in this way is that you can select the exact stations and/or markets in which you wish to advertise your product. This also allows you to customize the message to each location, so that if you have a chain of muffler shops, you can mention the address or phone number of each one in each market's ad.

Some stations are linked together only for the purpose of selling advertising time. They constitute an "unwired" network, allowing you to select which stations within the group you wish to use based on your demographic or geographic preferences. Typically, an advertiser buys time through a representative, or rep firm, rather than dealing with every station individually. So if you are trying to target teens with a new video game, you could go to a rep firm that offers you stations that do well against that group. Examples of unwired networks include the Baseball Network, which is popular among men, and the Concert Music Network, which offers classical music and performs well against adults over 25. Again, for the advertiser, using a network of this kind provides you with a single invoice for all of the stations. But, as with wired network radio, you may end up buying time on less-attractive stations as part of the package deal.

Benefits of Radio to Advertisers

As an advertiser, you cannot afford to ignore the many benefits of radio advertising. Although it does not offer the visual power of television advertising, it does provide the opportunity to reach targeted audiences frequently, at a reasonable cost. These and other benefits of this medium are discussed below.

Local Appeal

As we mentioned earlier, most advertising dollars in radio are spent at the local or regional level rather than on the networks. Radio is therefore listened to primarily as a local medium, allowing you the opportunity to tie in to local events, news, or celebrities.

Reaching the Right Audience

Because of the way radio stations are formatted, the medium provides you with targeted, specific audiences. If you run a local health club, you can reach women 25 to 54 by placing your message on light rock stations. Or, as the owner of a religious bookstore, you can promote your store by advertising on the local religious radio station. Radio also offers good opportunities for reaching ethnic groups. In areas with sizable Black or Hispanic populations, you are likely to find at least one station that appeals to each of these minorities. It will generally have a very loyal following. For a baby-clothing manufacturer, for example, advertising to Hispanics may turn out to be very profitable because they tend to have larger families than non-Hispanic households.

Keeping Costs Down

Compared with television, radio is an extremely inexpensive ad medium. A 30-second spot in prime time on a broadcast TV network may run as high as $200,000, while the price for that same length commercial on a local radio station will be closer to $11,000. Of course, these costs are linked to the number of people you will be reaching.

Building Frequency

With a TV buy, you are usually looking for high reach numbers. In order to gain frequency, you need either a very large budget or inexpensive dayparts. On radio, however, because the costs are so low, it makes sense to buy a lot of time and build up frequency against your target audience. It also makes sense to do this for strategic reasons; people tend to listen to a particular station for a fairly brief period of time, so you want to ensure you reach them while they are listening. You should keep in mind that listening habits are not seasonal, so frequency can be built up year-round.

Radio and Purchasing

Research shows that the time between media exposure and purchase is shorter for radio than for any other traditional medium, as shown in Exhibit 4.11. This means that your potential consumers may well be listening while they are making their purchase decisions.

EXHIBIT 4.11   Time between Media Exposure and Purchase

Radio	1.48 hours
Outdoor	2.54 hours
Television	2.54 hours
Newspapers	3.24 hours
Magazines	3.42 hours

Flexible Messages

Compared to the high production costs and long lead times of television, radio is extremely flexible. If your ad is read live on the air, as is often done, you can change the message at very short notice without much difficulty. You can also vary the message for different dayparts or station formats, perhaps using different music backgrounds depending on the type of music played on that station. Radio also offers the flexibility of tie-ins to local retailers or other promotional opportunities, such as local contests or events.

Drawbacks of Radio Advertising

In addition to the numerous benefits of radio advertising, there are a few drawbacks to keep in mind, as well. Each of these can be seen as challenge; most can be overcome with some planning and creativity.

In the Background

When we listen to the radio, we are usually doing something else at the same time, making it a background medium. Ads on radio must therefore work a lot harder to grab—and keep—our attention.

Sound Only

Radio can only offer sound, rather than the sight and motion of television. However, the medium can still be used to great effect because it offers the possibility of inspiring the listener's imagination. You can hear the waves crashing against rocks, or breaking glass, or party chatter, and conjure up images in your mind of what the scene looks like. Radio advertisements also tend to feature humor fairly often both as a way to get attention and because the audience is less likely to be distracted by any visuals and can listen to the words.

Short Message Life

Because we listen to radio in the background, for the most part, ads on this medium have a very short message life. Like TV, and unlike newspapers and magazines, once the ad has aired, the opportunity for exposure has disappeared. This makes it all the more critical to grab the audience's attention right away with a message that is relevant, involving, and interesting.

Fragmentation

One of the more recent drawbacks for radio is the fragmentation of the medium. We no longer just have "country" stations, but there are "hot country," "young country," and "traditional country" formats, among others. Each one appeals to slightly different kinds of people so if you wanted to reach them all, you would have to buy each type of country station in a market. Audience shares, particularly in major markets, may be very small, which makes it hard to use the medium as a reach vehicle.

All the News That's Fit to Print— Newspaper Advertising

Newspapers are one of the oldest media forms in this country. They were also one of the earliest media to accept advertising. In fact, the first advertising agencies were established to handle the purchase of space in this medium. Some of the earliest ads were for "medicinal" remedies, such as Lydia Pinkham's Compound.

In contrast to many other countries which have national newspapers, in the United States, newspapers are written for and distributed to a primarily local audience. As a result, most of the advertising is placed on a market-by-market basis. You can also choose which section of the paper to appear in, such as news (local, national or international), sports, entertainment, business, fashion, food, home, and travel, among others.

There are currently 2,488 newspapers published in the U.S. This figure includes both weekday and Sunday editions (1,613 and 875, respectively). That number has remained relatively stable during the past 250 years. In 1970, for example, there were 2,349 papers published. Newspaper audiences are measured in terms of *circulation,* or the number of people who subscribe to or purchase the newspaper. Exhibit 4.12 shows the top ten papers across the country based on their circulation.

EXHIBIT 4.12   Top Ten Newspapers by Circulation

Rank	Newspaper	Circulation (000)
1.	Wall Street Journal	1,819
2.	USA Today	1,495
3.	New York Times	1,141
4.	Los Angeles Times	1,090
5.	Washington Post	814
6.	New York Daily News	764
7.	New York Newsday	748
8.	Chicago Tribune	691
9.	Detroit Free-Press	556
10.	San Francisco Chronicle	544

Source: DDB Needham Worldwide Media Trends 1994. Data provided by Audit Bureau of Circulation.

The past decade has witnessed a decline in the percentage of the adult population that says they read a paper daily. Currently, about 61 percent claim they do so, in contrast to the 78 percent who read a paper back in 1970. What is even more worrying for the newspaper industry is that the readership figure is lower among younger people, who will constitute the medium's future readers.

Another problem the industry faces is the demise of the two-newspaper town. Most large cities used to have at least two competing newspapers; today, due to the high costs of running a newspaper, that is the exception rather than the rule. Only in the largest cities (New York, Los Angeles, Chicago) are there still two or three daily papers. This not only harms the newspaper industry, it is not particularly good news for advertisers either. Without competition, the paper can set its advertising rates wherever it wants them, as long as it can still compete with other media alternatives.

Newspaper Advertising Revenue

The largest part of newspaper advertising revenue (52 percent) comes from retailers. This includes large companies, such as major national department stores like JC Penney and Sears, to regional banks like Bank of Boston or BancOne, down to Joe's shoe repair shop around the corner. Second in importance as far as newspaper ad revenues are concerned is classified advertising (35 percent). The most important classified sections are for real estate and automotive, which together account for the majority of classified ad dollars.

The third type of newspaper advertising is that which is placed on a national basis so that it appears in all (or most) papers across the country. This type of advertising represents only 13 percent of total advertising revenues for the medium, despite the efforts of many newspapers to position themselves as valuable national vehicles in the face of increased competition with other local media, such as spot TV and radio, regional magazines, or billboards. The main problem that advertisers have with using newspapers on a national basis is the considerable premium that it costs to run their ads in all markets. Most are reluctant to pay that premium, which can cost up to 75 percent more than a local or regional ad.

Newspapers also offer a medium within a medium, in the form of *free-standing inserts,* or FSIs. These are pre-printed sheets, most of which carry coupons, that are usually distributed within the Sunday paper. On that day, too, most newspapers carry a special magazine supplement, either produced by the paper itself or coming from one of the nationally syndicated Sunday supplements, *Parade* and *USA Weekend.*

Benefits of Newspapers to Advertisers

As Exhibit 4.12 illustrated, the top ten newpapers in the United States reach nearly ten million consumers every day. Add to that the circulations of the other, smaller, newspapers in the country, and you'll begin to see just what kind of exposure is possible with newspaper advertisements. But, in addition to reach, newspapers offer advertisers a number of important benefits which are discussed below.

Timeliness

The day after the stock market crashed in 1987, ads appeared in many newspapers reassuring consumers and stockholders that everything was still alright. Johnson & Johnson was able to respond equally fast after the Tylenol poisoning scare of 1985. Unlike magazines or even television, newspapers are by their very nature filled with "news." People turn to them for the latest information on products, prices, and availability. The role that newspaper advertisements play in purchase decisions may be critical. A recent survey found that 70 percent of all newspaper readers agreed with the statement that "The paper helps me to decide where to shop and buy." And 65 percent felt that the newspaper was more important than television in making purchase decisions. In addition, electronic scanner devices in most supermarkets and retail stores are now able to assess the link between advertising and sales more directly and rapidly. Data suggest that newspaper ads can triple the sales volume for items that are advertised at reduced prices.

Desirable Audience

In the battle to attract advertisers, newspapers can offer highly desirable audiences. A newspaper reader is more likely to be better educated, have a higher income and be more involved in upscale activities than non-readers. People with a household income of $40,000 a year or more are more likely to be newspaper readers. Exhibit 4.13 gives a profile of the newspaper audience.

EXHIBIT 4.13 The Newspaper Reader

Professional/executive
Graduated or attended college
Age 35+
Working full-time
Household income $40,000+
Suburban
Largest county size
Married
Own home

Source: Mediamark Research, Inc., 1993.

In contrast to other media, readers spend a considerable amount of time with the newspaper. In 1987, the average length of time given to reading the daily paper was 45 minutes. And on average about two-thirds (67 percent) of all newspaper pages are actually opened, a figure that depends in part on the number of pages in the issue. In thinner papers (10 to 32 pages), 78 percent of all pages are opened, but when the paper becomes much bigger (81 to 204 pages), only 63 percent are opened.

Another consequence of the time readers spend with the paper is that it offers the media specialist more opportunity to provide detailed information. If you are trying to sell a new home equity loan program, you need the space to provide details on the terms of the deal, as well as on bank locations so interested consumers can find you. While you might worry that so much fine print will be boring or encourage page-turning, those people who are in your target audience will probably be interested enough to read through the entire ad (assuming the copy is inviting and attention-getting).

Impact of Editorial

An obvious advantage of newspaper advertising is that you can choose which section of the paper your ad is placed in, putting food ads in the Food Section, or offering investment advice in the Business pages, for example. This effectively narrows your reach to those consumers most likely to be interested in your product or service.

Local and Regional Possibilities

Although advertisers are reluctant to use newspapers on a national basis, they rely on them heavily for local or regional marketing. If Procter & Gamble wishes to test a new detergent in Peoria, Illinois, it can advertise in the *Peoria Journal Star* and feel confident that the message will only reach those people able to buy the product, thereby creating awareness for the new item. They might also test the effects of advertising on sales this way. For regional operators, such as Rax Restaurants—located only in the northeastern part of the country—ads can be placed in newspapers in the selected markets where the restaurant is found.

Even within a market, an advertiser can buy space in only those papers being sold in a certain area. The *Chicago Tribune,* for example, offers 21 zoned editions of its daily paper.

Drawbacks of Newspaper Advertising

As with every medium, newspapers have their own drawbacks as well as benefits. The three most critical drawbacks of newspaper advertisements are short issue life, the challenge of grabbing the reader's attention, and the constraints of using a largely black and white medium.

Today or Never

While magazines can often prolong their issue life and reach more people by being passed around or picked up on several occasions, at the end of each day the newspaper is usually discarded. If the reader misses your ad that day, you are not given a second chance. So, although newspapers are available every day, their issue life is very short.

Active Readers

The issue life of the newspaper is closely linked to how people read it. For although more than half of all pages are likely to be opened, it is up to the reader to actively choose what to look at. If your headline doesn't attract Jane Doe's attention, she won't look at it at all; if the copy isn't intriguing and relevant to her, she can simply turn to another article or page. It is therefore crucial that newspaper advertisements get the reader's attention. When people sit in front of the television or listen to the radio, they are generally a "passive" audience with no choice but to attend to the ad (even if fleetingly) or turn off the radio or T.V. set. Exhibit 4.14 shows how the newspaper advertiser must fight for attention.

EXHIBIT 4.14   Getting the Newspaper Reader's Attention

Size of Ad	Percent of Ads Read on Opened Pages
Less than one-quarter page	12%
One-quarter to less than one-half page	17
One-half to less than full page	25
Full page or more	44

Black and White

Until a few years ago, it was rare to find a color ad in a newspaper. Then along came the Gannett Corporation with its national newspaper *USA Today,* which offers full-color capabilities. The quality of newspaper color reproduction has been improving ever since, although it is still a long way from looking as sharp as magazine pages (due primarily to the poorer quality of the paper it is printed on). Even so, newspapers charge a premium for use of color, generally about 17 percent extra for a one-page four-color ad. For many advertisers, particularly those who wish to show "lifelike" qualities such as food manufacturers, it remains more effective to use magazine or television ads.

Magazines—An Explosion of Choice

Although magazines have a long history in the United States, with the earliest publications appearing in the middle of the eighteenth century, they are also a medium that may be said to have had two very distinct life stages. Originally, most magazines catered to a very general audience, offering a mixture of news, stories, and features aimed either at the total population or, in the case of titles such as *Ladies' Home Journal* and *Good Housekeeping,* at women. The strength of publications such as *Life, Look,* and the *Saturday Evening Post* is reflected in the fact that an ad placed in those magazines in the 1950s would be likely to reach about 60 percent of the total population.

But with the rise of television in the 1950s, general interest magazines found they could not compete effectively either for advertising dollars or for readers. Rather than simply disappearing, magazines began to move towards greater specialization in their targeting and their editorial content. This trend continues today, with extremely narrowly focused magazines devoted to topics such as tropical fish (*Tropical Fish Hobbyist*), cross-stitching (*Simply Cross Stitch!*), or aircraft (*Affordable Aircraft*). And while there are still some general offerings, including the resurrected *Life* and *Saturday Evening Post,* their readership is but a shadow of what it once was. Because of this increased specialization, there are today more than 2,000 different magazines available. In 1992 alone, nearly 700 new titles were introduced.

Magazines Today

Despite this specialization, magazines as a medium reach a broad range of the population. Indeed, 94 percent of all adults read magazines in any one year, seeing on average 9.6 different issues in that time period. Moreover, each magazine copy is looked at over 3.2 days, with the reader exposed to each page, on average, 1.7 times.

There are three main types of magazines available: Consumer, Farm, and Business-to-Business. Consumer magazines are usually categorized according to their editorial content, such as business, men's, women's, sports, news, and entertainment. This category includes titles enjoyed by all segments of the population, from *Time* to *Sports Illustrated* to *Cosmopolitan.* Farm magazines are geared towards that particular industry. Some may be crop-specific, such as *Cotton Farming,* while others deal with the technical aspects of agriculture. The third type, business-to-business, covers all titles aimed at the industrial user, everything from *Chemical Age* to *Offshore Drilling* to *Information Week.*

Taken together, magazines account for 6 percent of all ad dollars spent in the United States. Most magazines are considered as national vehicles for advertising, although there are numerous city or regional publications within the consumer segment, such as *Milwaukee* or *Southern Living.* More and more, however, national magazines offer geographic breakouts of their circulation allowing an advertiser to place a message that will, for example, only reach southerners, or people living in the northeast states, or in the Chicago metropolitan area. They are also developing more demographic "splits," so that Fidelity Investments can advertise its mutual funds in the edition of *Business Week* that is read by people earning $75,000 or more per year.

As with newspapers, magazines are assessed in terms of their circulation. Today's top circulation magazines are shown below.

EXHIBIT 4.15   Top Ten Magazines by Circulation

Rank	Magazine	Circulation (000)
1.	Modern Maturity	22,399
2.	Reader's Digest	16,258
3.	TV Guide	14,614
4.	National Geographic	8,165
5.	Better Homes & Gardens	7,601
6.	Family Circle	5,072
7.	Good Housekeeping	5,012
8.	McCall's	4,602
9.	Woman's Day	4,520
10.	Time	4,335

Source: *DDB Needham By the Numbers Cost Guide 1994/95,* based on Standard Rate & Data Service.

Magazines are sold in one of two ways—at the newsstand or by subscription. For most titles, it is the latter that generates the most sales, typically accounting for 80 percent of a title's circulation.

Benefits of Magazines to Advertisers

To an advertiser, three of the most attractive qualities of magazines are their high-end audiences, the enthusiasm of those audiences, and the long issue life of the medium.

Upscale Audiences

One of the incentives to using magazines for your advertising message is the favorable demographic profile of magazine readers. Similar to newspaper readers, the heaviest user of this medium is in the age range of 18 to 44 years, with a college education and household income over $50,000, and living in a household of three or more people.

Getting Attention

Another benefit of placing your ads in magazines is reader involvement. While this concept is rather difficult to define (and even harder to measure), it generally refers to the interest that the reader has in the material, both editorial and advertising. Since most magazines today focus on a particular subject or interest, they can tie in more readily with the personal needs and lifestyles of the audience, enabling advertisers to do so as well. In this way, automakers can target car enthusiasts or prospective buyers in *Car and Driver* or *Road and Track;* detergent manufacturers can promote their new or improved products in magazines aimed at homemakers (*Better Homes and Gardens, Good Housekeeping, Ladies Home Journal*); while financial services companies can offer their mutual funds to interested investors in *Fortune* or *Money.*

Consumers also seem less resistant to seeing ads in magazines. One study conducted by Audits & Surveys in 1986 found that whereas 82 percent of those surveyed felt there was too much advertising on television, only 54 percent felt similarly about magazines. Indeed, two-thirds of those surveyed *preferred* that magazines carry ads. And while 73 percent found television commercials distracting, only 34 percent said those in magazines were. This is in part due to the fact that as a reader, you get to select what ads you read, whereas with television the ads are more or less forced upon you (the remote control notwithstanding).

Reactions of readers to magazine ads also differ to their reactions to ads on television. Information seen in magazines tends to be retained longer because people can read up to five times faster than they take in the spoken word. They tend to trust magazine ads more, placing greater faith in the authority of the printed word. And in many instances, reading a magazine can be considered a pre-shopping experience, allowing your consumers the chance to compare products and services and learn new information about your engine oil prior to purchasing it.

Hanging Around

Another important, and unique, feature of magazines is their *long issue life.* While the television program is over in half an hour, and the newspaper is thrown out after one day, you will probably keep a monthly magazine in your home for four weeks or longer. This not only gives you opportunities for additional or repeat exposures to the advertising, it is also likely that other people, known as the *secondary* audience, may see the issue, too. The importance of this *passalong* readership is shown by the fact that the average magazine is seen by four different readers, with each one spending about 61 minutes with the issue.

Drawbacks of Magazine Advertising

Magazines, too, have their drawbacks. Among the most significant obstacles to keep in mind are the considerable lead time necessary and the relatively high cost of reaching your targeted audience.

Long Planning Cycle

For most publications, ads have to be completed and at the printer well in advance of their publishing date, a factor known as the *lead time*. This makes it difficult for advertisers to create particularly timely or newsworthy ads of the kind seen in newspapers. Moreover, despite the generally excellent color reproduction quality, the magazine remains two-dimensional (aside from pop-up displays or inserts, discussed further below). This prevents the magazine ad from offering the truly lifelike qualities of a television spot.

Reaching Readers

The increasingly targeted nature of magazines means that the cost of reaching one thousand members of the audience (the *CPM*) is higher than that of a broader, mass medium such as television. Even some of a magazine's benefits can be viewed also as potential disadvantages for you as a media specialist. The notion of readers' involvement with the magazine also means that, if they are not very interested in a particular product or ad they can very easily ignore it by simply turning their attention to the next page.

Outdoor Billboards—From Cairo, Egypt, to Cairo, Illinois

There are some in the outdoor industry who like to claim that billboards are the oldest medium in existence. They date it back to Egyptian times, when hieroglyphics were written on roadside stones to give people directions to the nearest town or village. Whether you agree with that or not, outdoor billboards are certainly well established, having been around in this country since the 1800s. At that time, companies began leasing space on boards for bills to be pasted (hence the term *billboard*). There are two main types of billboard—poster panels and painted bulletins. Panels come in several sizes, named according to the number of sheets of paper originally needed to cover them, such as 8-sheets and 30-sheets. Posters are found mostly in populated areas, such as in or near cities and towns. Painted bulletins are larger boards situated along highways and major roads. Their name refers to the fact that they were originally painted by hand at the site.

Putting messages on outdoor boards used to be extremely labor-intensive. The sheets for poster panels were pasted onto the board while bulletins were hand-painted. Both were created either at the board site or at a central location within the market or region. Since this had to be done in each market, differences resulted in the look of the message from one market to another (and even one site to another within the market). Today, thanks to computer technology, most poster panel messages are created electronically and then shipped either in one piece or in sections to the board site. Bulletins still tend to be hand-painted, but computers are now used to make sure that the finished product looks identical across boards. Today, bulletins are often created using other materials, such as lithography or special stretch vinyl.

In the past 30 years the industry has come under increased criticism from environmentalists who claim that the boards are a blight on the scenery. Many cities and several states have introduced bans on putting up new boards and, in certain cases, demanded the removal of existing structures. So you won't see any billboards in Hawaii or Vermont, for example.

Unlike other media which have editorial material too, outdoor billboards exist solely for advertising messages. They are primarily a local medium, bought on a market-by-market basis, but are used by both national and local advertisers. The type of business using the medium has changed considerably in the past 20 years. Although the biggest category of advertiser is still the tobacco industry, the proportion of sales it is responsible for has been falling steadily in recent years. Today, you are far more likely to see billboards from local retailers, the travel industry, or healthcare providers than you would have even five years ago.

Benefits of Outdoor Billboards to Advertisers

The advantages of billboard advertising have contributed the medium's popularity over the past two centuries. Four of the most consistent and important benefits are size, mobility, effective reach, and cost. Each of these advantages is discussed below.

Big is Better

Simply the size of the poster panel or painted bulletin means that outdoor advertising gets noticed. In fact, at a typical busy location in the center of a city, more than 10,000 people are likely to pass an 8-sheet poster panel within a given month. In addition, the message is there constantly, for 12 to 24 hours (and many posters are illuminated at night).

Mobility

Not only can painted billboards be moved around an area to expose more of the target to the message, but the outdoor messages can be designed for specific locations, audiences, or activities. So you could place ads for luggage aimed at businesspeople at airports to catch them when they travel, or advertise particular food products near the supermarket where your target audience shops.

Reaching Ethnic Groups

With outdoor billboards you can tailor your message to members of a particular ethnic group using their own language or culture yet still reach a mass audience within a specific market. You can buy space in areas with heavy concentrations of Hispanic people, for example, reaching them where they live, work, and shop. It is harder to reach a large portion of these groups with traditionally "Anglo" television or magazines. Furthermore, it is valuable to be able to reach nonnative English speakers in their first language, whatever language that might be.

Reinforcing the Message

Outdoor advertising is a good supplementary medium, helping to add reach and frequency to a media schedule at reasonable cost. A fairly typical outdoor buy could reach over 80 percent of adults in a given area in a month. In addition, the fact that the billboard is there all the time means that frequency builds up and the message can be a constant reminder. Because many panels are situated in shopping areas, an advertiser can present his message very close to the point of purchase.

Drawbacks of Outdoor Billboard Advertising

In considering what part of your advertising budget to commit to outdoor billboard advertising, you will need to keep in mind the two drawbacks of the medium: short exposure time, and the potential for criticism from environmentalists.

Brief Message Exposure

Since the average outdoor message is only seen for between 3 and 7 seconds, the copy needs to be extremely concise and compelling. For products that need a lot of explanation, outdoor is clearly not the right medium. One way to gauge whether you have too much copy to put on a billboard is to estimate how quickly people are going to pass by it. Or try the exercise yourself on existing panels, and see how much of the message you can take in as you drive or walk by. Because most of the viewing is done at high speed, especially for bulletins situated along the highway, the advertisement must also be eye-catching and interesting enough to attract the driver's (or passenger's) attention.

Environmental Criticism

The outdoor industry, as noted earlier, has come under increasing criticism for cluttering up the environment. Advertisers might shy away from the medium to avoid legal or ethical disputes, especially in areas with a recent history of environmental controversies.

Which Media Should You Use?

Now that you have some basic information on each major media category, we can start to consider why you might or might not wish to include them in your media plans. To make this process less cumbersome, we'll need to recap some of the most important advantages and disadvantages that each medium offers. These are summarized in Exhibit 4.16.

EXHIBIT 4.16 Pros and Cons of Major Media

Medium	Benefits	Drawbacks
Television		
	True to life	High cost
	Everywhere	Brief exposure
	Reaches masses	Ad clutter
Radio		
	Local appeal	Background message
	Targeted audiences	Audio only
	Low cost	Brief message life
	High frequency	Fragmented
	Close to point-of-purchase	audience
	Flexible messages	
Newspapers		
	Timely	Brief message life
	Desirable audience	Active readers
	Editorial impact	Weaker color
	Local/regional flexibility	capabilities
Magazines		
	Upscale audiences	Long lead time
	Reader involvement	Higher CPMs
	Long issue life	
Outdoor Billboards		
	Larger than life	Brief message
	Ethnic targeting	exposure
	Supporting medium	Environmental impact

Non-Traditional Media

As the traditional media forms outlined above grow increasingly cluttered, advertisers are looking for new and different ways to present their messages to the target audience. Two of the most important means available are Yellow Pages and in-store advertising.

Yellow Pages

Although placed under non-traditional media, Yellow Pages advertising has been in existence for almost as long as the telephone directory itself. Offering advertisers (and consumers) another type of classified advertising, the Yellow Pages generated $9.5 million in advertising revenues in 1993. There are more than 6,000 different Yellow Pages directories in the United States, which can make it harder for advertisers because of the lack of standardization in terms of ad sizes or guidelines.

People use the Yellow Pages to look up information and services. More than one-fifth of the time, the search is related to business needs. The top three categories that people turn to are food, dining out and entertainment, and automotive. According to Mediamark Research, Inc. (MRI), about one-quarter of the population has used the Yellow Pages in the past seven days. Within the past few years there have been some new developments in Yellow Pages advertising. First, the industry has attempted to attract more national advertisers, who accounted for just 15 percent of total revenues in 1993. But for consumers, the Yellow Pages are usually considered a means of finding local information.

Now, in many markets, you can not only see the name of the business or brand on the printed page, you can also hear about it on the phone. This is done through an audiotext service that allows you to call a local phone number and obtain information on a wide variety of services or topics simply be entering a four-digit code. The advertiser sponsors an audio message that is played before you hear the information in which you are interested. So, if you call up to hear the weather forecast, you might first hear a message from Joe's Heating and Air Conditioning, reminding you to have your heating checked out before the cold weather arrives.

In-Store Advertising

Just like Yellow Pages advertising, the notion of placing advertising messages inside stores is not especially new. Signs and promotions have been available in stores for more than 25 years. Today, however, more and more advertisers are including in-store media explicitly in the media plan, acknowledging this media form as advertising rather than simply a promotional expense. One of the main reasons for its increased popularity is that it is the most measurable of all media. Thanks to electronic scanning at the cash register, advertisers are able to see what happens at the checkout counter when their messages are in the store. Some of the most popular locations for in-store messages are on the shelves and in the aisles. In addition, messages or coupons can be generated at the checkout counter when people pay for their goods, tailored to the purchases that have just been made.

In-store advertising effectively eliminates the time between seeing the message and buying the item. Drawbacks include the possibility that the target misses the ad somehow, either by not paying attention or by its being covered up in some way. In addition, in-store advertising is not especially cheap. It tends to have its greatest affect among current brand users rather than persuading buyers of the competitor's brand to switch. The time for message exposure is very short, so messages tend to focus on price and be extremely brief.

Summary

Before deciding which media might best be suited to achieving your plan objectives, it is important to consider the advantages and disadvantages that each type of media can offer. Issues to be included in your analysis include the reach and/or frequency of the medium, length of message exposure, audience involvement, clutter, targetability, and cost. For each media category, an examination of the benefits and drawbacks will help determine whether—and to what extent—it should be included in the final plan.

Checklist—Exploring the Major Media

1. Do you want primarily national or local media in your plan, or a combination of both?
2. Will the benefits of television (mass reach, closeness to reality, and pervasiveness) help achieve your media objectives?

3. Have you considered the drawbacks of television (cost, brief exposure time, advertising clutter, and uncertain pod positioning)?

4. Will the benefits of radio (local appeal, targeted formats, low cost, high frequency, and message flexibility) help achieve your media objectives?

5. Have you considered the drawbacks of radio (its background nature, audio-only message, brief exposure time, and fragmented market)?

6. Will the benefits of newspapers (timeliness, editorial affinity, local and regional capabilities, and upscale audiences) help achieve your media objectives?

7. Have you considered the drawbacks of newspapers, such as brief exposure, poor color capabilities, and selective readers?

8. Will the benefits of magazines (upscale audiences, involved and interested readers, and long issue life) help achieve your media objectives?

9. Have you considered the drawbacks of magazines (long lead time, two-dimensional message, and higher costs per thousand)?

10. Will the benefits of outdoor billboards (large message size, rotating message, ethnic targetability) help achieve your media objectives?

11. Have you considered the drawbacks of outdoor billboards (brief message exposure and environmental impact)?

12. Are there opportunities to use Yellow Pages or in-store advertising in your media plan, to increase the impact of and audience for your message?

CHAPTER FIVE

Terms, Calculations, and Considerations

Defining Key Media Terms

Just as computer programmers talk about bits, bytes, and RAM, and car enthusiasts dwell on RPM, jerk, and lateral acceleration, so do media specialists converse in their own language. Before moving on to the actual media plan development, it will be helpful to review some of these definitions.

Understanding Ratings

Most of you are probably already familiar with the weekly release of the Nielsen ratings that show which are the most popular television programs. The size of the audience is usually given in two ways—in absolute terms (i.e., millions of people), and as a percentage of the population. It is this latter figure, known as the *rating,* that is used as the baseline measure for all media concepts.

Rating Point

One rating point equals one percent of a particular target group. That audience can be defined in various ways—by household, by geographic market, or by a given demographic group, such as men 18 to 49 or women 25 to 54, or by product usage or ownership, such as people who own a 35-millimeter camera. The television program "Home Improvement" might receive a household rating of 15.3 in Memphis, which means that 15.3 percent of homes in that city watched the show. The magazine *Macworld* might get a rating of 6.7 among male computer owners, meaning that 6.7 percent of all men who own computers read that particular issue of the magazine.

Gross Rating Points

By adding up all the rating points we wish to achieve, we end up with a concept known as gross rating points, or GRPs. For media planning purposes, we set as our goal a given number of total, or "gross" rating points to achieve and then figure out which vehicles to use to obtain that number. We might want our plan to have a total of 100 gross rating points each week against our target of working women. These could come from any media.

The reason these rating points are considered "gross" is that they do not take into account any duplication of exposure. That is, there are probably many people within our target who see our ad for lawn fertilizer in *Gardening Today* and also hear the same message on the local talk radio show. So while our total number of rating points placed in the media each week is set at 100, each person will be exposed to a different number of them and in different vehicles. This is shown in the diagram below.

EXHIBIT 5.1   Diagram of GRPs/Duplication/Vehicles

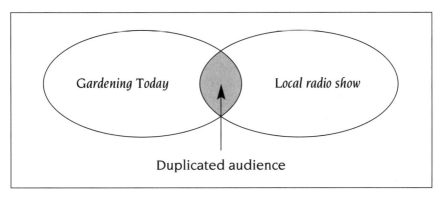

In today's complex media world, where our targets are becoming more and more narrowly defined, the term GRP is often altered to TRP, or "target rating point." This makes explicit the fact that we are planning our ratings against a specific *target,* rather than the whole world. The concept is the same, however.

Gross Impressions

This term simply converts the gross rating points into a number by dividing the number of rating points by 100 and multiplying that figure by the size of the target audience. So if our plan calls for obtaining 200 GRPs against a target audience of 500,000 people, then we are aiming to achieve 1,000,000 gross impressions (200/100 × 500,000).

Reach and Frequency

Although many would argue that advertising is more art than science, we still need some way to assess whether the messages we place in the media are having any impact. It is not enough to know how many impressions are made with one ad, or what percentage of the target audience is exposed to a given program or magazine. As media specialists, we also need an estimate of the cumulative effect of our media plan. That is provided by the concepts of reach and frequency.

Reach

Reach refers to the number or percentage of people in the target audience who will be exposed to the medium where the message appears. You should note that we can only estimate exposure to the *media vehicle,* not to the ad itself. If you think about your own media habits, there are many intervening variables that easily prevent you from seeing or hearing an ad. You might deliberately ignore it, turning the page of the magazine or changing the TV channel when it appears. You could be doing something else at the same time, such as talking to a friend or cooking dinner, and not pay attention to the message. Or you could find the ad boring, irrelevant, or uninteresting, and see or hear it but not really absorb the contents. So when we talk about the reach of a plan, we are really talking about the opportunity-for-exposure (sometimes called opportunity-to-see, or OTS).

And of course we should also emphasize that reach, like all media terms, is merely an estimate. We will never know exactly how many people were reached, or how they reacted. But if we are trying to reach women 25 to 54 to persuade them to try our new brand of furniture polish, then using syndicated data sources, we can find out how many women of that age view "All My Children," or read *Soap Opera Digest.* To reach a target audience of men 18 to 49 to increase the number of inquiries for our mutual fund company's pamphlet on investing wisely, we can learn how many men of that age read a daily newspaper, or watch the Cable News Network.

The difference between reach and GRPs is that reach concerns the number of *different* people in the audience you are trying to communicate with through advertising. For media schedules that try to maximize reach, you would place ads in several different media vehicles to reach different people through each one. Complicated formulas are used to calculate the numbers, requiring the speed and power of computers. Here, we look at a simple example.

If the rating for *TV Guide* against our target of 18 to 49 year olds is 20 and for *Time* magazine it is 15, then one ad placed in each magazine will deliver a total of 35 GRPs (20 + 15). However, if we know from research that 6 percent of the target audience will see both ads (the duplicated audience) then the reach, or *unduplicated* audience for this schedule is 35 – 6, or 29 percent. That is, 29 percent of our target of adults 18 to 49 will be exposed to our ad in *TV Guide and/or* our ad in *Time*. Even if they see both ads they will only be counted in our audience one time. Exhibit 5.2. depicts this situation. So reach = GRPs – duplication.

EXHIBIT 5.2 Reach and Duplication

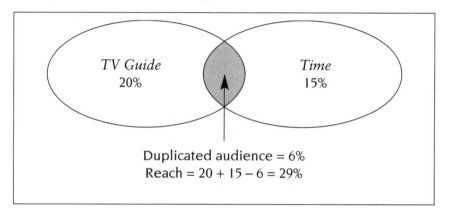

Duplicated audience = 6%
Reach = 20 + 15 − 6 = 29%

Frequency

It is not enough to know who our media plan is intended to reach. We must also set goals of *how many times* we wish to reach them with our message. As with the concept of reach, the notion of frequency, while it ultimately refers to *message* frequency, in reality is based on the frequency of exposure to the *media vehicle* rather than to the advertisement. A media plan will typically establish the desired number of times that the audience should be exposed to the message, based on past experience, judgment, or previous research into how long it takes for the audience to comprehend and remember the message.

A simple way to back in to the frequency number is from the following equation:

$$\text{Reach} \times \text{Frequency} = \text{Gross Rating Points}$$

So if you know your reach goal, and you have established the number of GRPs you will be buying, then it only requires simple mathematical division (GRPs/Reach) to figure out how many times, on average, the target will be exposed to the media vehicle(s).

Beyond Reach and Frequency

If you think about the commercials that you can remember, the ones that are most likely to come to mind are those that you have seen or heard more than once. That is, for a message to be truly *effective* in terms of communicating with the target audience, it generally has to be conveyed more than one time. Now of course this is not a hard-and-fast rule. If your bathroom drain gets blocked up, then you only need one exposure to an ad for Drano drain cleaner at the right moment in time, and that message will be extremely effective. But for the most part, given the limited attention we pay to commercial messages, we need to see or hear them several times before the information is properly absorbed. And even then, it is most likely filed away somewhere in memory for use on a future occasion.

Effective Frequency

The key here is to determine *how many times* an ad has to be received for it to be deemed effective. What we mean by effective is that the target receives the desired communication message. A considerable amount of research was done on this topic during the 1970s and 1980s, following a landmark study by Colin MacDonald, a British researcher. After looking at the relationship between opportunities to see ads for laundry detergent and sales of the product, he concluded that the optimal number of exposure opportunities was three. This was later explained by breaking down what happens with each exposure. The first time someone sees an ad, his reaction is "what is it?" On the second exposure, he asks "what of it?" or "so what?" It is only on the third occasion that the person will start to process the information and decide if the message is relevant and interesting or not.

Since those research studies were first published, there has been much controversy over their accuracy. Many have argued that it is impossible to set an arbitrary number for effective frequency. Some believe that rather than having a single figure, the most effective frequency lies within a range, typically set between three and ten. But others have correctly pointed out that even this is too restrictive. As with the drain cleaner example above, sometimes a single exposure is sufficient. On the other hand, you might need to see an ad for a breakfast cereal 15 times before it has any real impact. What it ultimately depends on is the relevancy and impact of the message.

The key point to remember here is that when establishing your media objectives and deciding on the strategy to fulfill them, you must keep in mind that your message should probably be heard, read, or viewed several times in order for it to have an effect on the audience.

Exposure Distribution

Most media plans involve placing multiple ads in many different media vehicles so it is important to know how many people are reached how many times (once, twice, three times, and so on). We find this by creating an *exposure distribution,* which shows the percentage of the target exposed to a given schedule at each level of frequency. The method used to calculate it is fairly complex, based on mathematical theories of probability, and today it is generally done by computer. At a basic level, a media model estimates the likelihood of being exposed to a given number of ads together with the number of different ways you can be exposed to those messages.

For example, if you placed one ad in *Time* and one in *TV Guide,* the reader might see anywhere from zero to two ads total—they might not see either ad, or they could see one of the two, or they might see both. Looking at Exhibit 5.2, we already know the percentage of the target exposed two times (the duplication figure) is 6 percent. In addition, we can easily figure out those not exposed at all (the total, or 100 percent, minus those exposed one or more times)—100 – 29 = 71 percent. So to estimate what percentage is reached exactly once you subtract the duplication figure from the number reached one or more times (*reach 1+*)—29 – 6 = 23. You should notice that the final exposure distribution must account for everyone in the target audience and therefore sum to 100 percent. The final exposure distribution is shown in Exhibit 5.3.

EXHIBIT 5.3 Exposure Distribution

Frequency (f)	Percent Reached
0	71
1	23
2	6
	100

Calculating Costs

It is highly unlikely that your client or boss will give you *carte blanche* to spend however much money you want or need. They are going to want some kind of financial explanation of how efficiently your plan will spend their money. And since there are many different media types and vehicles that could, potentially, be included in the plan, it is up to the media specialist to rationalize and explain the financial reasoning behind selections.

Cost per Thousand (CPM)

Since different media are bought in different ways—a 30-second spot on radio or TV, or a one-page ad in a magazine, or a 30-sheet poster for a billboard, we need some way to compare media in terms of cost. To do so, media specialists turn to the cost per thousand, or CPM. This shows the cost of reaching 1,000 of the target audience either with an individual media vehicle or the complete media schedule. It puts all media on a level playing field and is calculated as follows:

CPM = Total Schedule Cost/Gross Impressions (000)

Let's use an example of 120,000,000 adults 18 to 49, and assume that an ad in *TV Guide* costs $120,000, while one in *Time* costs $143,000. For a schedule using one ad in each magazine with a total of 40 GRPs, 48,000,000 impressions would be generated. At a total cost of $263,000, the cost per thousand would be $5.48. This means it costs $5.48 to reach 120,000,000 adults age 18 to 49 with one ad in *TV Guide* and one in *Time* in a given month. By using this formula, you can compare the cost efficiency of one vehicle, media category, or schedule against another.

Cost per Point (CPP)

Another useful media tool is the cost per rating point (CPP), which offers a different way of comparing media schedules. Here, you find the cost of one rating point for each media vehicle against your target by dividing the total schedule cost by gross rating points:

CPP = Total Schedule Cost/Gross Rating Points

With our total cost of $263,000 and total rating points of 40, the cost per point comes out to be $6,575. It therefore costs $6,575 to obtain one rating point against adults 18 to 49 using one ad in *TV Guide* and one in *Time*. If you know the cost per point against a particular target group and the approximate number of rating points you wish to buy, you can then calculate an approximate total schedule cost, using the same formula.

Category-Specific Criteria

In addition to knowing the general terms that are used in media planning, it is helpful to be familiar with some of the other criteria that are used in selecting each major media category. The rest of this chapter will outline these considerations.

Considerations for Television Advertising

The chief currency for a television plan is the program rating. As we do not measure audience exposure to the actual *commercials*, we have to rely on the surrogate number of how many people watched the *program* in which it ran. That data is available from A. C. Nielsen Company, for both national and local markets. If you or your agency do not subscribe to these services, the TV station or network can supply you with the appropriate figures.

The U.S. TV marketplace operates based on the laws of supply and demand. The more people who watch a particular show, the more expensive it is to advertise within it. The ranges are enormous. You might pay $300,000 or more for a 30-second commercial on network television during prime time, but only a few hundred dollars to have your ad appear on your local TV station during the night. That cost will correspond to the number of people exposed to your ad—millions, versus a few hundred.

In addition to the costs and ratings, it can be helpful to look at the Viewers per Viewing (or Tuning) Household, or VPVH numbers (sometimes called VPTH). This figure provides you with an assessment of the concentration of a given demographic group in a program's audience, showing how many people in every thousand viewers fall into that particular category. So if the VPVH among women 25 to 54 for "All My Children" is 535, and for "This Week with David Brinkley" it is 155, that indicates you will reach more than three times as many women 25 to 54 with an ad placed in the soap opera than you will with the weekly news show.

What you should be most interested in, as a media specialist, is finding which programs are going to best reach your target audience. As we noted in Chapter 3, although you may have a fairly detailed description of your customer, when it comes to getting data on TV audiences you will end up looking primarily at age and gender. Since those are very powerful determinants of product purchase and behavior, for many goods and services those numbers will suffice. Until the industry finds an affordable and reliable way of measuring TV viewing according to product usage patterns, it is likely that program ratings among broad demographic groups will remain the norm.

In selecting your programs, you should keep in mind that the list may be changed when the commercial time is bought. The plan is just that—a *plan* of which media vehicles are desired. When negotiations take place, it may be that other programs are included, or some of your recommendations rejected, based on other considerations such as cost and availability. What you should emphasize, however, is the *daypart* that you wish your ads to appear in, for although people do tend to watch individual programs rather than time periods, there is more similarity in the kinds of programs watched within time periods than across them.

The criteria you use to evaluate which programs to use for television do not vary whether you are planning to use network, spot, syndication, or cable. If you are planning on a local level, however, there is additional work to be done. You must select the markets to advertise in (if you have not done so already) and, more particularly, the stations within those markets that you want to use. That will depend in part on the negotiations that are done by the media buyer. That process is explained more fully in Chapter 8.

For cable TV, you may have to rely on broad network information rather than specific programs. Individual cable shows tend to have much smaller audiences (ratings) than do shows on network or spot TV. But those audiences may be more finely targeted due to the "narrowcast" nature of this form of television (see Chapter 4).

Considerations for Radio Advertising

Radio uses the same principal term as television for planning and buying purposes. That is, you purchase time based on audience ratings. The main difference here is that the rating is based on a time period, rather than on a program. For the most part, you plan radio by dayparts (which were given in Chapter 4), although it is possible, for an additional cost, to specify selected, narrower time periods. For example, if you operate a chain of local restaurants and only want to advertise in the hour before lunch (which technically falls in Morning Drive), you could request the Noon-to-1:00 P.M. hour, and most stations will sell that time to you, though perhaps at a premium.

Radio audiences are measured by The Arbitron Company, and reported on a quarter-hour basis, so you can look at the Average Quarter Hour (AQH) rating for each station in a market. This is the average number of people listening to an individual station for at least five minutes within the quarter-hour period, expressed as a percentage. In many larger advertising agencies, the media planner only specifies the markets to be used, leaving it up to the media buyer to choose the actual stations, based on his or her own knowledge of those markets.

The market itself can be defined (and measured) in several ways. The largest geography is called the Designated Market Area, or DMA. It is defined as the viewing or listening area in which the counties that have the stations of the originating market get the largest share of household viewing or listening. Every county in the United States is assigned to just one DMA.

A smaller geography for radio is the Total Survey Area, which consists of the metropolitan area, plus outlying additional counties that listen to the major metro stations. In Chicago, the Total Survey Area would not only include the Chicago metropolitan area, but also the rest of Cook, Lake, and DuPage counties, which can also receive Chicago radio station signals. The most narrowly defined measure is the Metro Survey Area. This is in fact defined by government according to the city and surrounding counties which are closely linked economically to the central city area.

The total radio listening figure is provided in the Persons Using Radio (PUR) measure, which is equivalent to TV's Persons Using Television, or PUT number. This tells you what percentage of a given audience are listening to radio at a particular time.

If you are purchasing radio time yourself, another measure that is worth considering is the Time Spent Listening, or TSL. This gives an indication of how much time people are spending with an individual station in a daypart, day, or week. The calculation is as follows:

$$\text{TSL} = \frac{\text{Number of quarter-hours in daypart} \times \text{AQH}}{\text{Total Listening (Audience)}}$$

The more time people spend listening to that particular station, the greater the chance of reaching them with your message. On the other hand, if your goal is to reach as many *different* people as possible, then the TSL may be of less concern.

The media specialist should also consider the *cume rating,* which is the total number of people listening to a particular daypart, expressed as a percentage. And finally, to find out how quickly a station's audience changes, you can calculate or ask for the audience *turnover* figure, which is the ratio of total number of people listening to a particular station in a daypart to the average number listening to that station in a quarter-hour. If the turnover is high, meaning that people don't listen to the station for very long at any one time, then that would suggest you would need to air your ad fairly frequently in order to reach more people.

An increasingly important area of consideration for radio is merchandising and promotion. Many stations are very willing to organize special contests or announcements or "added value" events if you buy time from them. If you operate an ice-cream store franchise, for instance, perhaps you could arrange for the station to hold a contest, with the prize being an ice cream party for the winner and his family. For a local cable television company, a radio station could agree to air additional announcements and public service messages, in return for being mentioned on the local access cable channel. A car dealership might provide the perfect venue for the radio station to send some of its disk jockeys on the road for an afternoon, airing the program from the actual showroom. All of these "extras" can be negotiated for little or no additional cost, yet they provide valuable "free" advertising for you and your company. Moreover, because they are organized on a local basis, they help to enhance your firm's place in the community, offering you some image-building public relations, too.

For network radio, the terms used are the same, but here you must consider which of the networks to include in the plan. Again, at larger agencies this is often left up to the buyer (where planning and buying are separate functions), based on demographic or format specifications.

Considerations for Magazine Advertising

Some of the criteria to consider when planning for magazines include coverage, composition, circulation, subscription, rate base, readership, positioning, and discounts.

- **Coverage.** Just as for the other media forms, the coverage tells you the proportion of a given target group that saw (were 'covered' by) the publication in the past month, or whatever is the relevant publication period.

- **Composition.** This number will show you how concentrated a magazine's audience is with a particular target group. It can be useful in providing the media specialist with some idea of how well the publication will reach your particular audience. If you are trying to advertise an answering service to small businesses, it would be important to know what proportion of the readers of *Home Office* and *Entrepreneur* run their own businesses. While the one-page cost or the CPM may be cheaper in *Home Office* than in *Entrepreneur,* if you are going to reach more small-business owners who would be interested in your service in *Entrepreneur,* then the cost of reaching one thousand of *those* individuals would in fact be less expensive.

- **Circulation.** It is important to look at how many copies of the magazine are circulated for each issue. This information is either provided by the magazine itself in an audit report or can be obtained from the Audit Bureau of Circulation, the premier source for circulation data. New or very small magazines may not be audited by this independent organization; if that is the case, be wary of relying on the estimates the publisher provides as they cannot be verified. When looking at circulation, the media specialist should also find out what proportion of that figure is *controlled*—distributed free of charge to potentially interested parties. They are usually not the main target audience for the publication and, therefore, would be less interested in seeing the ads that appear. In addition, you should look at the *net paid* circulation figure, which gives you the number of copies sold at no less than half of the basic newsstand or subscription price. Circulation is also usually broken out by geographic area, which can be very helpful, particularly for products that have regional skews.

- **Subscription or single copy.** Another valuable number is the percentage of copies that are sold by subscription versus on the newsstand (single copies). If people are getting their copies sent to them every month, that might suggest they are particularly keen to keep receiving and reading the magazine; on the other hand, the argument could be made that the single copy reader renews her commitment to the publication every time she purchases an issue. Whichever side you believe, it is worth finding out how the subscriptions are sold, and at what price. Publishers are able to discount subscriptions very heavily (up to 50 percent) and still consider them a full subscription. If the price is very low or there are enticing premiums offered for people who buy a year's worth of the magazine, it could well be that the person who receives that title is more interested in receiving the free personal stereo or CD than in looking at your ads.

- **Rate base.** Finally, you should find out how many times in the past six months or one year the publisher has not met his guaranteed audience size, or rate base. This is the number of copies that he promises the advertiser he will sell. Although the advertiser does not get anything back if that number is not reached, a magazine that consistently fails to meet its rate base is probably one you should avoid. This information is provided by companies such as the Audit Bureau of Circulation, that measure circulation on a regular basis. The magazine publisher should also release that data upon request.

- **Readership.** For those who have access to syndicated services, there is a wealth of additional information available on reading habits for individual consumer magazines. This includes factors such as the average number of days a title is read, the average number of minutes spent with the publication, where it is read, what actions were taken after reading it, and how many readers saw each copy. These qualitative data are summarized in Exhibit 5.4. They may be provided by the individual publication.

EXHIBIT 5.4 Qualitative Magazine Data

> Where read
> Bought versus obtained
> Days spent reading
> Time spent reading
> Actions taken (clipped coupon,
>   sent away for information, etc.)
> Rating of publication
> Interest in advertising

Armed with all of this information, the media specialist can then compile a list of preferred magazines to use in the plan. Clearly, the cost of the ad page will also be a crucial factor in determining which individual titles are selected.

- **Positioning.** There is conflicting evidence concerning where it is best for your ad to be in a magazine. Some studies have shown a clear advantage for being at the front of the issue or on the cover page, while others suggest there is little difference in terms of likelihood of being seen. Positioning will also depend on the publication. For some magazines, such as *Cosmopolitan* or *Newsweek,* most of the feature articles appear in the first two-thirds of the book. But for more specialized magazines, such as *Computerworld* or *Object-Oriented Design*, readers may also be extremely interested in the smaller ads at the back of the issue which feature products or services for the computer enthusiast.

- **Discounts.** A few years ago, all magazine ads were bought off a rate card that specified exactly how much an ad would cost per issue. While discounts were given for placing ads in several issues, there was little room for any negotiation. In today's highly fragmented media world, magazines have been forced to become more competitive, both between titles and against other media. One positive result of this, for the advertiser, is that magazines are far more willing to negotiate discounts or special deals now than they were previously. An advertiser who places a large *volume* of ads (and, therefore, dollars) in a magazine will get a special deal, as will advertisers who build up frequency or continuity with the publication. There is also a slight discount for cash payments. It is always worth checking with the magazine's representative to find out if there are ways to lower the unit cost.

Considerations for Newspaper Advertising

If newspapers are to be included in the media plan, the first consideration is which markets are to be used. The list of markets can be developed based on population or household size, on sales data of the product, or on CDIs and BDIs. A list created according to population may be a simple ranking of the markets (top 10, top 20, and so on), or it could be a ranking based on the target audience (top 10 markets where the target is located). Market lists that are based on sales data will tend to emphasize those places where current sales are occurring, while one derived from CDI or BDI figures will also factor in potential future opportunities.

In looking at the individual markets, the media specialist needs to have a clear understanding of the product's distribution within those areas. Is it available primarily within certain parts of the market, or ADI? Is it found more in the metro area or the suburbs? Are there any major ethnic areas of the market that could play a role in product or media usage?

Once you have determined which markets to use, there are three main criteria to consider for newspaper planning: circulation, coverage, and readership.

- **Circulation.** As with magazines, the newspaper circulation figure tells you the number of actual copies that are distributed. This figure is used to compare one paper with another, as well as give some idea of how many coupons might potentially be distributed. Circulation is often broken out into counties or city zones, depending on the size of the market. While one newspaper might have a larger overall circulation, another might deliver more readers in the particular zone where your retail outlet is located and therefore be a more appropriate vehicle to use.

- **Coverage.** The coverage number, also called the newspaper penetration, is the print equivalent of a TV rating. That is, it shows the percentage of households reached by a given newspaper. As with the circulation figure, the numbers might look different depending on how the coverage is defined. Taking Boston as an example, if you only consider the overall market, or ADI household penetration, you might choose the *Boston Globe,* but if you are interested in reaching singles, or Blacks, the *Boston Herald* has greater coverage.

- **Readership.** Newspaper readership figures provide more detailed information about the paper's readers according to standard demographic breaks or, where available, product usage data. Using these numbers, the media specialist can find out what proportion of the readership is 18 to 49, for example, or how many readers are working women. One newspaper may reach more men than women, or more younger adults than older ones.

  The media specialist can use all three criteria to compare different newspapers both within and between markets, as well as help determine which individual papers will do the best job of reaching the given target audience. In markets where there is more than one newspaper available, it is also important to find out how much duplication there is of readers to both vehicles. It could be that one is aimed primarily at the city and the other is read mostly in the suburbs, or that Paper A reaches the northern section and Paper B is preferred in the south. Your selection of individual or multiple newspapers will depend to a large degree on the geographic areas that you wish to cover.

Considerations for Outdoor Advertising

As with newspapers, the main decision to be made when including outdoor boards in a media plan is which markets to select. Once that is known, the media specialist must determine which kind of outdoor board to use—poster panels, or bulletins. In either case, the unit of sale is the showing. It is typically sold as a 25, 50, 75, or 100 GRP showing. The number refers to how many panels or boards are required to reach that proportion of the market. A 50 GRP showing, for example, means that your ad will appear on enough boards to reach 50 percent of the total population daily. This is completely market specific. Generally, the outdoor company will provide you with the information on how many boards make up each showing size.

Audience delivery estimates are usually also made available by the company that owns the boards, or can be obtained from the Traffic Audit Bureau, which conducts the independent measurement of traffic past those sites.

Summary

In this chapter, we covered some of the basic terms and features of media planning. In order to understand media, it is essential that the media specialist be familiar with the concepts of reach, frequency, gross rating points, and gross impressions. Beyond these, it is also helpful to understand the notion of effective frequency, which assumes that in order for an ad to be effective, the target audience has to be exposed to it more than one time. An exposure distribution lets you know the number of people who are exposed a given number of times to an individual vehicle or a complete media schedule. Media costs are accounted for by calculating the cost per thousand (CPM) and cost per rating point (CPP).

The remainder of the chapter looked at various considerations for each major media category. For television, this includes the program rating, audience composition, viewers per viewing household (VPVH). Radio plans need to examine the time spent listening, cumulative rating, and audience turnover. When magazines or newspapers are included in a media plan, it is important to know the publication's circulation, rate base, and actual readership. Finally, the main consideration for outdoor is planning the appropriate showing level to reach a given proportion of the target audience with the correct number of billboards.

Checklist—Terms, Calculations, and Considerations

1. Have you figured out how many gross rating points your schedule will deliver?

2. What is the reach, effective reach, and average frequency of that schedule?

3. If you plan to include television in the schedule, have you looked at both program ratings and viewers per thousand viewing household (VPVH)?

4. If you plan to include radio in the schedule, have you looked at the average quarter-hour (AQH) ratings, cume audience, time spent listening and turnover for each station?

5. If you plan to include magazines in the schedule, have you looked at the coverage, composition, circulation, rate base, ad positions, and discounts?

6. If you plan to include newspapers in the schedule, have you looked at the coverage, circulation, and audience composition figures for each paper?

7. If you plan to include outdoor billboards in the schedule, have you looked at the GRPs available in each market being considered?

CHAPTER SIX

Creating the Plan

Putting together a media plan represents the culmination of all the thinking, planning, and organizing that we have discussed in earlier chapters. That is, with sound advertising and media objectives, a knowledge of who it is we wish to reach with our messages, and a clear idea of what different media can offer us, we are now in a position to start assembling the plan. The key idea to keep in mind when doing this is your *media strategy*. What is it you are hoping to achieve by using media vehicle X as opposed to Y? How will your combination of media categories and vehicles help fulfill your advertising and media objectives? As with any process, there are several steps to the creation of the plan. These are outlined in this chapter.

Target Audience's Use of Media

The first step in building the media plan is finding out which media your target audience uses. There is not much point in putting your Super-Kleen message on hundreds of radio stations across the country if the 25-to-54-year-old adults you are trying to reach tend to be heavy television viewers. You can discover the media habits of your potential customers through syndicated services such as Mediamark Research, Inc. (MRI) or Simmons (SMRB), or through custom studies that you conduct or solicit on your own. The third alternative, which is the cheapest but may be less accurate, is to do some mini-research on your own. You might want to start asking your clients or customers where they have seen your ads; if you have been advertising in the local newspaper for years but nobody mentions it, then that might indicate the need for a different medium.

By this point, given what you now know about what each media type can offer (and what it can't), you are probably starting to see how the various media will fit in to your particular strategy. So if your goal is to increase awareness of your beauty salon's new manicure and massage treatments, you might turn to the media best suited to that awareness goal—television and magazines. On the other hand, if you want to increase the frequency of visits to your pizza restaurant, then local radio might be a better bet because you can place a large number of ads at a reasonable cost and keep repeating the message to remind listeners of your establishment.

As you start to assemble your media categories and vehicles you also need to think about several other considerations—the timing of the plan, its scheduling, and its geographic variations. We consider each of these in turn below.

Timing of the Plan

For many products, the timing of the plan is self-evident. That is, you want to advertise snowblowers in winter and sunscreen in summer. Other items are tied in to specific days or weeks of the year, such as

Valentine's Day candies or Thanksgiving turkeys. But for the majority of goods and services, you would ideally want to promote them continually, getting your message out on a very regular and frequent basis to reach as many people as you can as often as possible.

There are two obvious drawbacks here. First, for most advertisers, particularly small businesses, they simply cannot afford to do this. And second, there are good reasons *not* to bombard the media constantly with your message. People are going to tire more quickly of your ads, making them tune out or ignore them sooner. They may even grow so irritated by seeing or hearing them all the time that they actually develop less favorable opinions of your brand or company. Most of all, there is no point advertising something unless you have something worth saying. Remember, an advertising message has got to tell the consumer about something that they will be interested in. If all you did was place a message in the paper or on the radio 365 days of the year saying "I'm here," you would be unlikely to see much effect, if any, on your sales.

You need to focus your efforts on particular months, weeks, or days. Deciding when to do so is not all that difficult. Most businesses have some seasonality to them, even those that are used or frequented all the time. You probably know, for example, that people stock up on office supplies at the end of the financial period (quarterly or semi-annually); they flock to health clubs at the start of the New Year and when the weather begins turning warmer. Apartment leases tend to be signed in May and October, making the rental business busy just prior to those dates.

You might want to use one of two tactics here. Either you could focus your efforts on promoting your product right before the peak period, reminding people of your existence and trying to take additional share points away from your competitors. Or you could try to build up sales at other times of the year. Or you could try a combination of the two, maintaining a strong presence during the height of your "season," but also keeping a high profile at a couple of other times during the year, too. If you do choose to advertise when people may not be thinking about your product, then it is even more important that you tell them something new and interesting. Perhaps you lower your membership rates to the health club in March or October, and announce that in local newspapers and magazines. You need not be confined to "typical" seasonal patterns either. Maybe you can "create" an event for your business, such as an open house to your photography studio or a walk-a-thon to raise money for your nursing home. These kinds of special events not only provide you with excellent opportunities for self-promotion in the media, you can also generate additional coverage through public relations efforts and publicity.

It is also worthwhile considering the seasonality of the media you are planning to use. Most media categories have seasonal variations—the fourth quarter is often very tight, for example, because of pre-holiday advertising. For media sold on a supply-and-demand basis (radio and television), this can affect prices considerably. There are only a fixed number of minutes of commercial time available. Even for those media that have rate cards, such as magazines and newspapers, heavy media demand for space during those months may mean it is especially important to place orders well in advance.

Balancing Reach and Frequency

As you develop your media plan, it is important to keep track of how well it will perform. That is, you need to keep calculating your reach and frequency measures to compare one potential plan against another. The goal is to find the right medium, or combination of media, that will achieve your media objectives given the amount of money you have to spend. You can do so using the simple calculations shown in Chapter 5, based on the size of your target audience and the ratings of the individual media vehicles.

It may turn out that you will not be able to achieve the specific number you set as your goal for reach and/or frequency. In that event, you need to consider several possibilities. It may be that a 55 percent reach of the target is acceptable, even though you had originally planned to reach 65 percent, or that a frequency of three is all right when four was the ideal. And keep in mind, of course, that we are dealing here with plan *estimates* rather than actual reach figures. You may be restricted in the actions you can take. If your client demands that his message is seen on television, then that medium must remain in the plan. But perhaps you can opt for cable TV instead of broadcast, and, by reducing the cost, be able to place the message more frequently.

Alternatively, you might want to rethink your timing and scheduling strategies. Maybe instead of advertising every two weeks for six months, you could place your message every week for three or four months, concentrating your efforts on the most important period and increasing your reach and frequency within that time-span. Or maybe the addition of a third magazine will help boost the numbers, by reaching additional target members who are not going to see your ad in the two magazines you had first selected.

Scheduling Your Ads

You may have a good idea about when to start running your ads. The next question to think about is how to schedule them. Do you want them running each week for six weeks (continuity), or twice a month all year (bursts), or for alternating six-week periods (flighting)? The answer to this question will depend primarily on two interrelated factors: your media objective and your sales pattern. There should always be a timing component stated in your objective, which will give you some guidance for the scheduling of the plan. If you hope to reach 60 percent of your target during the next six months with the message that your print shop was rated number one in the city by a Chamber of Commerce survey, then you would probably disperse your ads throughout the period to reach as many different people in your audience as possible. For an accounting firm that wants to expose people to its message about its electronic tax filing capabilities, there would be good reason to schedule most of the ads in the three months prior to the April 15 tax deadline date, building up the frequency of the message at the time of year when it is most appropriate.

You should also think about the scheduling of different media, and their combination. Perhaps you could advertise your health food store in the local newspaper every week of the year, then supplement it with local cable ads around the time of each special promotion.

Much of what we know about scheduling tactics comes from our general knowledge on reach and frequency. That is, if you wish to reach as many *different* people as possible in your target audience, then you want to disperse your messages across media, vehicles, or days and dayparts, for example. On the other hand, if you want to ensure that your audience hears or sees your ads several times in a given period, you would concentrate them in fewer media, vehicles, days or dayparts.

The pattern of scheduling does not seem to make a difference, however, in terms of total reach. So whether your ads appear in two sequential weeks or alternate weeks (one week on, one week off), or are placed one week a month over four months, the final reach will be approximately the same. Of course, the timing element could be critical, depending on your product. It would not make much sense to spread ads for a highly seasonal item like suntan lotion or Christmas decorations across many months; but if you are promoting your dry cleaning business through newspaper ads, there is something to be said for having a fairly constant presence during the year (perhaps changing the message to tie in to the seasons or holidays).

Two television scheduling tactics that have become quite popular among major advertisers are *double-spotting* and *roadblocking*. Double-spotting refers to placing two spots within the same program. The effect of this technique is to increase the likelihood of multiple exposure to your ad message (i.e., increased frequency). Roadblocking means placing the same ad across as many channels as possible at the same time, so that when Joe Smith is watching television at 8:06 P.M. on a Friday night, whichever channel he turns to, he'll see the same ad. That is becoming harder and harder for advertisers to do as the number of available channels grows higher, making it a much more expensive proposition to undertake. The impact, however, is going to be an increase in reach, as your spot will be seen not only by Joe, but by everyone who was watching those other channels at 8:06 P.M..

Cost Efficiencies

Costs are obviously very important for the media plan. So, in addition to keeping track of reach and frequency figures as you create the plan, you must also consider the costs involved. Of course, these are closely related. If you need to increase the frequency of your message, it is going to require more media time or space, which means more money. But as we noted above, it might be possible to find a cheaper medium or vehicle to help your funds go further. Cost efficiencies can be calculated in terms of cost per thousand of the audience reached (CPM) and through cost per rating points (CPP). These were explained in Chapter 5. The more "mass" the medium, the cheaper it will be on a CPM basis, but the less targeted it will be for your situation. That is, there will be a lot of "waste" exposures of people who are probably not interested in what you have for sale. For a widely used product or service, such as car tires or a muffler shop, that might not be a bad thing. But if you are trying to reach a narrower group of people, such as Mazda Miata car owners, to offer them a specially designed luggage rack that sits on the roof of the car, then you would be better off with a higher CPM in a more targeted vehicle, such as car magazines.

Tactical Considerations

As you develop your plan, there are probably going to be numerous additional considerations that are specific to your product or service. These might include trade merchandising, consumer merchandising, and testing.

Trade Merchandising

For many goods and services, the trade plays a critical role in the brand's development and sales. Many media plans that are geared primarily to the consumer market also have some side benefits for the trade. When Frito-Lay promotes its Doritos corn chips, it is telling its distributors and retailers that it is pushing the brand and helping to increase their revenues too. A national ad for McDonald's restaurant is also designed to help the local franchisee. Even your ad for Super-Kleen furniture cleaner will reach professional furniture restorers or antiques dealers, in addition to the females 18 to 49 years old you are targeting.

In putting the plan together, therefore, it is important to look at what trade-merchandising elements may be attached to it. Perhaps if you operate a chain of regional oil-lube shops, you can bring all the operators together for a kick-off party when the media campaign begins. Even something as simple as buttons with your new campaign slogan can help give the trade a sense of being part of the picture. Sending them copies of the new ads and/or materials lets them know what message is being promoted to customers. The media can help here as well, particularly if you are one of their valued customers. They may be willing to co-sponsor an event for your distributors or retailers, for example.

Consumer Merchandising

Although we focus here almost exclusively on advertising media, it is important to keep in mind many of the other ways in which you can gain additional exposure for and mileage out of your media plan. There are a multitude of communications possibilities available, from coupons or sampling to press releases and exhibitions and displays. If you are promoting a line of gourmet preserves, then perhaps in addition to the magazine ads that you run, you can talk to the local grocery stores to set up sampling booths in their stores, and feature the dates and locations in the ads. For a computer dealer promoting the latest line of Macintosh computers, you could arrange to visit local schools and let the children play with the equipment, then call the local TV station and arrange for them to film it. The possibilities for these kinds of tie-ins, or what is popularly known today as "integrated marketing," are almost endless. Whatever you do, however, should remain within the overall communications objectives of your plan—increasing awareness, obtaining customer preference, encouraging brand selection, and so on.

To gain as much advantage as possible from consumer promotions, you might also consider increasing other media weight when a coupon is dropped, or placing more newspaper ads the week that you are sponsoring an open house at a local dealer, for example.

Testing

For most smaller advertisers, the notion of testing a plan may seem unnecessary. If you only have a few thousand dollars to spend, then it doesn't seem worthwhile. However, if you are about to change your entire marketing and media strategy, it is a good idea to see first—on a small scale—whether your new approach is likely to increase sales or harm them. For example, for a children's toy store that has traditionally only advertised in local newspapers to announce whatever was on sale that week or month, a change in strategy to increasing awareness of the wide range of items available might suggest a move into local television (cable or spot broadcast). The potential impact of such a media move could be estimated by placing a few of these ads and including some kind of response mechanism, such as a toll-free number or special deals to those customers who mention the TV ad. That way, the store could test how effective the TV ads are.

Testing is also a good idea for making changes in media weight (GRPs). If you are trying to persuade your client to increase annual spending from a few hundred dollars to several thousand, and you face resistance to the idea, then you might suggest a test of the proposed strategy in one or more markets, to see what impact those added dollars would have to the bottom line.

Presenting the Plan

Whenever you present your completed plan, whether it is to upper management at your own company or to your client, you need to keep two points in mind. The first is to *be visual*. Most people either hate or fear media because they believe it is a morass of numbers, most of which they don't understand. So the more you can do to present the information in ways that they can *see* what is going on, the better off you will be. That means using charts, graphs, pictures, photos, or video to liven things up and bring the numbers to life. For instance, if you are presenting the demographic statistics on your target, then perhaps you can make a short video that depicts these people in real life, or present charts or photos that demonstrate who they are.

The second point to remember is to *be brief*. Although you want to have all of the back-up materials and numbers to support what you are doing, when you make a presentation you should focus on the key points. Assuming you have an interested audience, they will look at the details afterwards or ask you questions as you go along. Again, the common perception of media is that it is a mind-numbing experience, filled with mathematical formulas and statistics that are, quite simply, boring.

Fortunately, there are ways around these problems. The first, keeping it visual, can be accomplished through the use of a flowchart. This can show, at a glance, when the ads will run, in which media and vehicles, at what cost, and to what effect (reach and frequency). It can be done for each target in a given plan, and be broken out by medium, if desired. An example is shown later in this chapter. There are numerous ways of creating a flowchart. You can simply draw one yourself, or use a spreadsheet computer program, or a custom media flowchart package (see Appendix for details).

Being brief is harder to do. It usually comes down to practice. Running through your presentation with a friend or colleague and asking for their advice can be useful. It is particularly helpful to present your work to someone outside of your area—if they can understand your concise explanations of media terms, then you are doing fine! Remember, however, to include all of the pertinent information (including calculations for how you arrived at your conclusions) in the deck of materials you leave behind. In addition, you have to show how your media plan fits in with and enhances the brand's marketing and advertising objectives and strategies.

Last but not least, it is crucial to remind your audience that you are dealing with estimates. Some of those may be informed by years of experience, but many are based either on your best judgment, syndicated data sources, or mathematical reasoning. People tend to believe that because you, as the media specialist, have placed a number on something, that turns it into "reality." If that were so, media planning would be completely automated and done by rote, a pure science, rather than the combination of art and science that it remains today.

A Media Plan Example

Let's go through an example for a fictitious brand of salad dressing, Salad Splash. This is a nationally distributed brand that was first introduced in 1988. It competes primarily with Kraft and Hidden Valley. Although it is available in a dozen different flavors and three different sizes, our plan focuses on Regular dressing.

Situation Analysis
Through the end of calendar year 1994, Salad Splash's sales are up 12% versus a year ago. This is the second year of double-digit sales growth.

Marketing Objectives/Strategies. Increase Salad Splash's penetration among frequent salad eaters in two ways:

- Year-round focus on salads, with
- Heavy-up during primary salad months (spring/summer).

Advertising Time Period. January through December 1995

Media Budget. $4 million

Promotional Activity. Free-standing inserts (FSIs) in mid-March and late-June.

(continued)

Marketing Background
Competitive Analysis.

- Kraft General Foods (KGF): Total spending: $15 million. 50% network television; 30% syndicated TV; 10% cable TV; 10% magazines.

- Hidden Valley (Clorox): Total spending: $12 million. 50% network television; 20% cable TV; 20% magazines (health, women's, food).

- Category total: Total spending: $136 million 40% network television; 25% magazines; 12% spot TV; 12% syndicated TV; 5% cable TV; 2% Sunday magazines; 2% national spot radio; 1% newspapers; 1% outdoor.

Seasonality. Salad Splash usage tends to peak in spring/summer months, but the product is used throughout the year.

Salad Splash

J/F	M/A	M/J	J/A	S/O	N/D
74	105	126	128	100	63

Salad Dressing Category

J/F	M/A	M/J	J/A	S/O	N/D
92	96	115	118	102	80

Advertising Objectives
1. Raise awareness of the convenience and flexibility of Salad Splash among target from current level of 40% to goal of 45% during calendar year 1995.

Media Objectives
1. Advertise to frequent salad eaters. The demographics and psychographics of this target are:

   - Women 25–54, Household Income (HHI) $40,000+
   - Well educated, professional or managerial, nutrition-oriented

   The target consists of 17 million women who can be defined as heavy salad dressing users (2+ bottles in last month). They represent 20% of all women.

(continued)

2. Achieve the following communication goals:

	Average 4-week Delivery	
	Peak period	*Rest of year*
	3+ reach	3+ reach
Women 25–54 with HHI $40,000+	45%	10%

3. Provide year-round media support to stimulate usage throughout year, with additional weight during the peak summer months.
4. Schedule advertising to run Wednesday-Sunday to complement key grocery shopping days.
5. Provide national advertising support.

Media Strategies

Following the success of the brand during the past two years, the 1995 media plan recommends a continuation of the media strategy, using cable television as the primary medium with magazines as the secondary medium.

Cable Television. As the primary medium, cable television provides:

- Immediacy of message.
- Demonstration of product in use.
- Broad reach.
- Cost efficiency.
- Continuity (due to lower cost).
- More upscale households.
- Added value programs (billboards, product mentions, contests).

The following cable networks are more likely to be viewed by the target:

- Arts & Entertainment
- Discovery Channel
- The Family Channel
- Lifetime
- Nick-at-Nite

(continued)

- USA Network
- The Weather Channel

Half of the cable weight will be in daytime, and the rest in prime time.

- Daytime offers more programming geared towards women.
- Prime time offers higher ratings, greater reach.

Magazines. As the secondary medium, magazines provide:

- Long message life.
- Repeat exposure.
- Opportunity for recipes, coupons.

Magazines will be divided between women's service (55%) and food (45%) magazines to:

- Generate additional reach in non-cable households.
- Effectively reach working women.
- Offer recipes and coupons.

All magazine ads will be 1P4C (one-page, four-color). Preferred position will be:

- Women's Service—Food section.
- Food magazines—Front of book.

The recommended magazines will include:

	Coverage	Index
Family Circle	31.6%	122
Good Housekeeping	28.3%	116
Cooking Light	4.0%	132
Prevention	9.3%	119
Redbook	14.8%	119
Woman's Day	25.7%	114
Bon Appetit	4.7%	124

The total cost of this plan will be: $4.2 million.

The following flowchart depicts how the plan would be laid out during the year.

(continued)

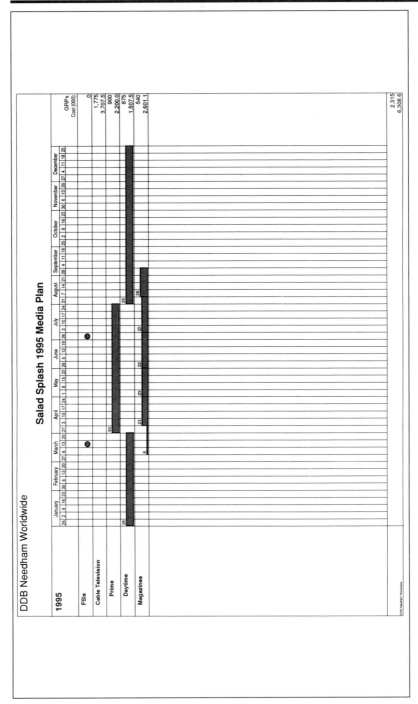

Source: Stone House Systems, Inc., 1994.

Although this is a very generalized and simple version of what to include in a plan, it provides the basic information that has been covered earlier in this book. You should note that all of the recommendations need to be backed up by research data, wherever possible, beyond simple tables showing indices or coverage for individual media vehicles or gross expenditures for the year. Here is a brief list of the kinds of analyses that could be included in the "back-up" for this plan:

- Media usage.
- Cable network comparisons.
- Magazine comparisons.
- CPM comparisons (e.g., cable versus other forms of TV).
- Cable/non-cable viewing analysis by daypart.
- Detailed reach and frequencies by medium.
- Media quintiles.
- Purchase volume for brand and category.
- Demographic analysis of users.
- Brand geographic analysis (BDI vs. CDI by DMA).
- Seasonality analysis.
- Grocery shopping patterns.
- Historical media plans.

Summary

When creating a media plan it is crucial to consider first the target audience's use of media, in terms of which categories and vehicles they use. You then must determine the plan's timing, if there are seasonal sales or other elements of the marketing mix (pricing, promotion, distribution or product changes) that will affect the plan's timing. For scheduling of your chosen vehicles, financial considerations and reach and frequency goals will help determine when, and how often, your ads appear. Tactical elements are important, too, particularly trade and consumer merchandising, to receive maximum support from dealers, distributors, and retailers, and maximize the impact of the advertising. If funds permit, or major changes to the plan are being contemplated, it is recommended that the plan be tested on a small scale before being launched in its entirety.

Checklist—Creating the Plan

1. Have you found out as much as possible about your target audience, either through syndicated services, or primary research you yourself conduct?

2. Have you determined the appropriate timing for your messages?

3. How will your messages be scheduled—continuously, in flights, or in bursts?

4. Will your reach and frequency goals be met by your timing and scheduling strategies?

5. Are there merchandising possibilities for your brand, with either the trade or with consumers?

6. Do you need to test the plan first in a smaller location before rolling it out?

7. Can you present your plan in a visually interesting and succinct fashion?

CHAPTER SEVEN

Offering Alternatives

O nce you have completed your media plan, you might think your task is over. But like the Energizer bunny in the popular battery commercials of the early 1990s, it keeps going, and going, and going. . . . In fact, even as you are creating the plan you should be starting to think about various alternatives. For, while you might be convinced that you have created the perfect, biggest sales-generating, best objectives-meeting media plan ever conceived, the chances are fairly good that it will not be accepted at face value. So rather than going into your presentation believing that your job is over and that the client will immediately accept everything you are recommending, you will be in a much stronger position if you prepare some alternatives beforehand. This chapter will consider what some of those options might be.

Spending More Money

The opportunity to gain a larger budget than you were originally expecting does not happen very often, and certainly not as often as a media specialist might like! However, there are several good reasons for being prepared to spend more on advertising media than was originally proposed. The first, from an agency perspective, is that if you are being paid a commission on the media you buy, the more money you spend, the more you will make. But second, and perhaps more importantly today when fewer and fewer advertisers are paying a 15 percent commission rate, it is your job as the media specialist to prove to the client how much more effective the media plan *could* be if there were more dollars available.

To some people this might sound purely wasteful. There is evidence, after all, to indicate that spending more on advertising may actually result in a *decrease* in sales! But for the most part, research supports the notion that placing more dollars in advertising media to reach more people on more occasions (assuming, of course, that they are the right people for your product) will increase sales. That won't occur in a vacuum; the other "Ps" of the marketing mix have to be working in your favor too. The product must be one that the marketplace needs; there has to be good distribution; and the price must be appropriate. But given those factors, increasing media dollars will tend to increase sales.

So, given those circumstances, how do you best prepare to offer the alternative of spending more? In many situations, the best way is to simultaneously create a second media plan that has a larger budget allocated to it. If your primary plan has an annual media budget of $500,000, then you might consider creating an additional one at the $750,000 level to see how that would perform. In doing so, you should not simply throw extra media weight around randomly. Instead, you should revisit your advertising and media objectives and consider what you might set as your goals if you had that extra money to spend. If, for instance, your original goal was to boost awareness of your home delivery shopping service from 25 percent to 35 percent in the markets where you operate, then perhaps if your budget was to be 20 percent larger, you might think about setting your objectives higher also, proposing that with the additional funds you could increase awareness to 40 percent in that same time period.

Another option with increased funding is to disperse your message across a wider area. If you have bookstores located primarily in three states, but are starting to expand into five additional states, then perhaps by spending more money on advertising media you could afford to put your messages into those new areas to let people know of your upcoming presence. Having more money might also allow you to branch out into additional media vehicles or forms. If your basic media plan for a carpet cleaning service consists of local newspaper and radio ads, then perhaps the extra dollars you are recommending be spent could permit you to buy local cable or spot TV ads.

Of course, in suggesting where and how this extra money could be spent, you must always show what will be achieved in return. That is, you need to quantify, wherever possible, the positive impact those dollars will have. This can be done through reach and frequency calculations that show how many additional people in the target will be reached, and how many more times they will have the opportunity to be exposed to the message. Supplementary funds may also end up *lowering* the cost of individual ads, either through volume or frequency discounts, or by reducing the cost per thousand (CPM). So although the bottom-line cost of the plan may go up, the cost efficiency may actually improve!

Another advantage to spending more media dollars is that they may allow you to reach a secondary target more readily. If you are putting a plan together for a company that makes lighting fixtures, where the primary target audience is construction firms, then perhaps expanding the plan will allow you to address more clearly a secondary target audience of individual contractors. You might also think about using additional dollars to reach people who can influence your primary target. For a media plan aimed at new parents offering a diaper service, you might spend the extra funds to promote your company to pediatricians and nurses to whom the parents will turn for advice.

It is also important to think beyond media when considering how additional monies might be spent. You might want to recommend undertaking some custom research of your proposed target audience, especially if that target has changed in some way from previous plans. Or research could be done to gain a greater understanding of how people use your product or service, or where they turn to for information about it that could, in turn, greatly enhance your media plans in the future. This could be particularly valuable if there is very little syndicated data currently available, or if you are in a very specialized or new field, such as computer biotechnology or electronic beepers.

And, of course, the people who actually create the ads would also like to have more money to spend on their work. Production quality could be improved, or commercials lengthened, or better talent hired if more dollars were made available. You could make your direct mail piece look far more professional, or distribute more samples to individuals visiting your exhibit at a trade show. The possibilities are almost endless. But whatever you recommend for your increased-spending scenario, you must justify it in terms of the objectives and strategies that you have stated upfront (even if you propose modifying those objectives if you get additional funds).

Spending Less Money

Unfortunately, for most media specialists, the more frequent case is that you will end up having to spend less than originally proposed. And while it is generally not a good idea to present to your client or boss a reduced-spending alternative at the same time as you present your main media plan (unless that has been specifically requested), you would be well advised to start thinking about how you would spend less money as you are developing the basic plan.

There are numerous reasons why you might end up having less money than you anticipated available for your plan. It could be that sales of your client's widgets fell more than they had expected this year, so marketing budgets for the coming year had to be cut (and remember, advertising is usually the first item to be cut when sales go down, despite the fact that those dollars will typically help *increase* sales). New management or ownership will often result in budgetary changes, and again, more often than not these changes are in a negative direction. It could be that the company decides to speed up the introduction of a new brand and decides to take money away from the established product for which you are preparing a plan.

Whatever the reason, as you are preparing an alternative plan think carefully about how you can put together a media schedule that will come as close as possible to meeting your original objectives. There may be several ways to cut corners without decimating the plan. Perhaps you can shorten the flight times, running TV ads for two weeks at a time instead of four, or only placing ads in magazines every other month instead of monthly. You must keep in mind, however, that by reducing your frequency you may end up losing some volume discounts with the media involved. And you will be likely to come up short on your reach and frequency goals.

Creating a reduced-spending scenario should not be a case of simply cutting spots or pages arbitrarily. It must be done with strategic reasoning in mind. For instance, let's say you have a media plan to get more parents in your area to consider sending their children to your client's preschool program, but instead of having $250,000 to spend, you end up having only $180,000. You had originally intended to send direct mailings to all parents of young children in the vicinity, inviting them to visit the school, as well as placing newspaper ads in community papers. Now, with less money to spend, you must reconsider how best to allocate your dollars yet still achieve your objective. Perhaps instead of using direct mail, which tends to be very expensive, you could try to get free publicity by sending a video news release to the local TV stations and media kits to other local media. An open house would also be an inexpensive way of offering parents the opportunity to visit the school. But in order to continue to reach a broad cross-section of people, newspaper ads would probably remain an efficient and effective medium.

Sometimes there is no alternative but cutting one or more media forms from the plan. Before doing so, it is important that you consider each one in turn, deciding what would be the result of eliminating that medium on the overall plan's objectives. This should not be limited to reach and frequency considerations, but also thought of in terms of what the medium can do for your ad and how consumers might react. If you take out all TV from a plan, then remember that you are losing the only medium which can offer sight, sound, and motion to your product. That might be less important for a car dealership, but critical for a hamburger restaurant where you want to show how delicious the food is.

Another way to reduce media spending is to use briefer or less expensive ads. Instead of 30-second commercials, maybe you could make do with half that time; instead of a full-page ad, perhaps a half-page will suffice. Once again, however, this must be considered not simply in numerical terms (such as reach, or CPM), but also in terms of the impact on consumers seeing or hearing that commercial message. Although some research evidence suggests that many consumers cannot tell the difference between a 15-second commercial and a 30-second one, there is obviously less time available in the shorter unit to tell the complete story, so you are missing out on the chance to reinforce your message as thoroughly.

It might seem appropriate, given a reduced media budget, to cut the size of your target audience and plan to reach fewer people. In fact, in many situations that can turn out to be *more* costly, for the more narrowly you try to target your media, the more expensive it becomes to try and reach them. If your original plan for a new cake mix is aimed at all women 18 to 49 and uses a mix of magazines and TV, then by trying to narrow it further to reach only those women 18 to 49 who have household incomes of more than $50,000 and have three or more children you will probably end up looking at more expensive media vehicles. Instead of picking a broadly popular woman's service magazine, such as *Good Housekeeping* or *Woman's Day,* you might end up with magazines that have a smaller circulation and cost more per ad page, such as *Gourmet* or *Bon Appetit.* Now admittedly, they *will* reach more of your more narrowly defined target, but the cost may be correspondingly higher, too.

One way you could consider making cutbacks on your targets is by eliminating any secondary targets you had planned to reach through separate media. A plan that was intended to increase awareness of an environmentally friendly detergent might be aimed at both environmentally aware consumers and opinion leaders. Faced with a cutback in media dollars, you might consider targeting only one of those groups initially, rather than both of them at once.

It is extremely important to outline the implications and results of spending less on advertising media. This should not be done in a gloom-and-doom fashion, portraying a picture of complete failure if $50,000 is removed from the budget, but neither should it be taken lightly and happily accepted without a fuss. If for no other reason, explaining what you believe might happen if those media dollars are removed will show to your client or boss that you have thought through in a strategic way the possible outcomes of alternative plans. Keep in mind that your ultimate goal is to get those media dollars restored as soon as it is feasible to do so.

Changing Targets

Sometimes after you have presented a complete media plan to the client and have apparently won approval for it, a little voice in the back of the room will speak up and say, seemingly casually, "But what would happen if we targeted X instead?" That simple sentence can send the alarm bells flashing and blood pressure soaring for the media specialist. It is important not to panic at that point, but rather, to think carefully about whether there is real merit to the question.

Although you may feel indignant that anyone is questioning your plan's target, particularly after all the work you have put into it, you need to step back and take a careful, considered look at the proposition. For as much as you may be reluctant to admit it, it could be that the person making the suggestion has actually hit upon a potentially valuable target which you had simply not considered or realized how important it could be. Sometimes it takes so long for the client and agency to agree on a single target, that once that definition has been pinned down there is a tendency for the media specialist to put on the blinders and work feverishly to deliver a plan with the agreed-upon target. Any considerations of alternatives have been set aside out of gratitude that the client has finally accepted at least one customer group. But as you are increasingly wrapped up in that target audience, the client may have time to sit back and ponder other possibilities, and may come up with one that is more appropriate, or equally so.

In the best scenario, that alternative target *is* in fact one that you had considered and rejected, either because of strategic or financial reasons. You can then explain why the different target would not be appropriate or feasible. If you had not already done so, then it is in everyone's interest to look more carefully at the proposed alternative (unless it seems so outlandish and unreasonable that you are certain there is no merit to it). It could be that a simple discussion then and there will be enough to determine whether this option should be investigated further. Or you may have to go back to syndicated research or whatever sources you were using to define the target and examine the proposed alternative more closely.

There are other situations where it is incumbent upon you, as the media specialist, to consider different targets as you are developing the primary plan. As noted above, this could be because you are creating alternative spending scenarios with more or fewer dollars available. But it might also arise because of disagreement or uncertainty over who the best target for the product is. Perhaps your bank client has always targeted its media plan to promote its mortgages at young couples looking for their first home. You, as the media specialist, might put together a second plan that targets older couples whose children have left home who want to move to a smaller, but more elegant home for their retirement, or are perhaps contemplating buying a second weekend home. Clearly, the media that you would use to reach each target group would be very different.

It could also be important to include different targets in a plan, or create a separate plan for those targets, when you think that there are critical secondary audiences who need to be addressed. This is highly dependent on the product category. For medicines or health-care items, for example, it is often essential to communicate with the medical profession as well as consumers, because they are the ones who influence which brands are selected. Similarly, for products targeted at children it is frequently advisable to have a separate target of moms or parents because they are the ones who typically hold the purse-strings.

Whoever the different target is, the media specialist must determine which different media are needed to reach those people. That, in turn, will depend upon the marketing and advertising objectives for that distinct audience—are they identical to the main target's goals, or do they differ in some way? How much do the two targets overlap, both in terms of those objectives and in their media usage patterns? It could be, for example, that if you are trying to encourage both consumers and contractors to select your brand of faucets, then certain ads placed in home decorating magazines would reach both groups, but more specialized trade publications will do a better job at convincing contractors of the merits of your brand, while TV ads could help enhance your brand's image among consumers.

Changing Media

As the media specialist, your job really entails considering different media from the beginning to the end of media plan development. You are doing so as you assess your media strategy and tactics and as you create the plan. However, it is sometimes worthwhile to make a special effort to consider how the plan would turn out if different media were used. Again, this could be in reaction to a change in the media budget, or a response to a client's or boss's question. Or you could take it upon yourself to investigate alternative media options.

In some cases, this could involve looking at different media vehicles within the same media form. If you are recommending magazines, then perhaps you might look at more specialized publications to reach your target. For TV, reconsider whether you should use network, spot, or cable TV to convey your messages. With a radio plan that uses spot markets, perhaps a network buy would be more efficient and appropriate. Or, if your media plan makes heavy use of newspapers, then think about whether you should move from small-town local newspapers to those that are distributed across broader regions, such as the *Boston Globe* in the New England area, the

Chicago Tribune in the midwest, and the *Los Angeles Times* in California. The use of different media vehicles will depend primarily on two factors: cost efficiency and targetability. It may be cheaper to use cable rather than spot TV, for instance, but if cable penetration in your area is only at 45 percent, then you are missing out on more than half of all the homes who could potentially be exposed to your message. Switching from smaller local papers to bigger, more regional ones may bring you a larger audience, but those people may not be close enough to your chain of healthy quick-service restaurants to be worth reaching with your message.

The bigger change when thinking about different media is a switch in media forms altogether. Instead of recommending newspapers, what happens if you use local cable TV instead? How about using network radio instead of cable TV? Or what would be the result of switching dollars out of magazines and into television? The media specialist must think through these scenarios both from the point of view of strategy and of cost. How would a move from newspapers to cable TV affect your overall objective of boosting awareness of your jewelry store? Would the same number of people be reached? Would they be the same people? What is the cost difference? And how would message frequency be impacted? What are the creative implications of such a change? All of these questions need to be answered as you develop a plan using different media.

The main idea to keep in mind when offering media alternatives is that your original plan is not the only way to schedule media to meet your client's marketing and advertising objectives. Here again we see that media planning is both art and science. There are potentially tens, if not hundreds, of different ways that you could plan your media to obtain the designated goals. Your job as the media specialist is to come up with the one that you believe will do the most effective and efficient job, while fully understanding that there are alternatives available that might achieve the same ends.

Tests and Translations

There are two common ways to conduct tests of a media plan on a local or regional basis. They are known as *As It Falls* and *Little America*. Here, we will consider the basic concepts for each one, rather than going through all of the mathematical calculations needed to prepare such a plan. Although this procedure is really a test, it is also sometimes referred to as a "test translation," to reflect the fact that a national or bigger plan is being recreated in some fashion on a smaller scale. And even though, as media specialists, we are most concerned with testing the media plan itself (increasing GRPs, trying different scheduling strategies, and so forth), tests are also often conducted to determine the impact of new creative, or to see how a new product fares in the marketplace.

As It Falls

This type of test is most often used for brands in existing product categories, where the competitors are well known. The main premise of this method is that the rating points are allowed to occur as they normally would in each market, or *as it falls*. So rather than have the same GRPs across all test markets, the plan's goals would vary somewhat from location to location, depending on how well the individual vehicles perform in each place. That also means that the budgets will vary by market, too. It may cost $2,000 to buy 100 radio GRPs in Boise, Idaho, but $5,000 to get the same GRP level in Madison, Wisconsin. The main advantage to this testing system is that it provides a realistic scenario for assessing the impact of the test plan. For if the plan were expanded to a national level, there would still be market-by-market differences similar to those seen in the as-it-falls test situation.

Little America

This test market procedure is used more often with new brands or products where there is no existing competition. What it sets out to do is recreate a national plan in one (or a few) markets, or get as close to that as is feasible. It usually involves more complex planning, first to determine how individual media categories perform in the markets you choose, and then to figure out how to adjust the test plan so that it matches the national delivery.

Summary

While creating a media plan, the true media specialist is already considering various alternatives. One that should always be included is a "what-if" scenario of the effect on the plan's outcome if more dollars were available, looking at the impact on cost efficiency, reach and frequency, and the marketing and advertising objectives. Increased funding could also be allocated to gain additional reach of the brand against its users, or improved production quality of the ads themselves. This chapter also examined a reduced-spending scenario, which must be undertaken with a strategic focus in mind, considering alternative media forms or vehicles, or fewer messages or targets. Indeed, plan alterations will frequently look at different targets or different media and estimate the impact those might have on the plan's effectiveness. All of these potential changes can be tested by translating the plan into a local or regional test market situation, and seeing what happens there first.

Checklist—Offering Alternatives

1. Have you prepared a second media plan at a higher budget level?
2. Have you considered how extra funds would be spent—longer flights, wider geographies, secondary targets—and how those would impact your media (reach and frequency) goals?
3. Are there non-media needs that require additional funds (creative requirements, consumer research, trade allowances)?
4. Do you know the impact of spending fewer media dollars on your plan—(fewer media categories or vehicles, reduced number of targets, reduced schedule, lower reach and frequency results)?
5. Are there other target audiences you should consider?
6. Are there other media categories to be considered?
7. Is it necessary to test your media plan first, either "as it falls" (existing brands) or in a "little America" (new products) test?

CHAPTER EIGHT

Making the Media Buys

E ven the most impressive media plan will not satisfy the client until the time and space have actually been bought. The role of the media specialist may involve none, some, or all of the media buying functions. This chapter provides a brief overview of how print and electronic media are purchased. The subject really requires book-length treatment on its own; the goal here is to show how media buying fits in with the planning process, rather than explain the many details and intricacies of the buys themselves.

Merchandising a Magazine Buy

In the plan for Salad Splash dressing, we included various magazine recommendations. It is increasingly common, even in large advertising agencies, for media planners to be responsible for magazine buys, although some agencies will have print specialists on staff who help in the negotiations. It used to be that all magazines worked off a *rate card,* listing the cost of buying various page sizes, with or without color or other special features. Additional charges were also made for preferred positions, such as the inside front or back covers and the back cover itself, which are believed to be read by more people.

While the extra costs remain, today's magazine buys are far more likely to be made by negotiating. That is, the rate card is usually the starting point, but then it is up to the media specialist and the magazine's representative (or rep) to discuss the final cost for the client. Discounts may be offered for volume buys if, for example, the client purchases ads in multiple issues, or buys several pages in one issue, or increasingly, buys space in several magazines owned by the same publisher. As we learned in Chapter 3, the cost of a magazine ad will depend also on the size and nature of the magazine's readership. Obviously, you will pay more to reach more people. It would cost you about $100,000 for a full-page, 4-color ad in *Ladies Home Journal,* which has a circulation of 5.2 million, whereas the same ad placed in *Vanity Fair,* which has a circulation of 1.1 million, will cost less than $60,000.

At the other end of the spectrum, however, you may also have to pay more to reach a highly specialized audience. Although both *First for Women* and *Southern Living* have circulations of 1.2 million, the one-page ad will cost $21,000 in the former and $71,000 in the latter because it is assumed that the more focused material of articles about the south is reaching a more interested, involved audience that is more likely to pay attention to the ads in that publication. There have been research studies both supporting and rejecting this hypothesis, with the dissenters claiming that if the reader is more involved in the subject matter, he or she is in fact *less* likely to pay attention to the ads. For the media specialist, the main focus should be on the suitability of each individual magazine to the media objectives, and how efficiently and effectively each vehicle can be used.

When the magazine space is negotiated, the specialist will usually request certain positioning preferences. As noted above, for some of these a premium must be paid. Aside from covers, the specialist may want a food ad, for example, placed near or within the food editorial, or a cosmetics ad to appear in that section of the magazine. Sometimes it is enough to simply request that the ad is in the first third of the issue, under the assumption that those pages are more likely to be seen. The willingness and ability of the magazine to fulfill these requests will vary, depending on who the client is and how many ad pages it needs to fill. One of the important things to remember about magazines is that, unlike electronic media, which have a finite amount of airtime, printed media (including newspapers) can simply add pages if they can attract additional advertisers.

In addition to the increased willingness of magazines to negotiate off the rate card, more and more publications are also offering additional benefits to their advertisers. These might include special promotions, editorial features, bonus circulation, or trade deals. While these are usually offered at little or no extra charge, obviously the cost is built into the amount the specialist pays for the ad pages. These extras reflect the extremely competitive media landscape, with an increasingly fragmented marketplace not only within the magazine industry, but also across different media. *Good Housekeeping* is no longer only competing with the other Seven Sisters books (*Better Homes and Gardens, Ladies Home Journal, McCall's, Family Circle,* and *Woman's Day*), it must also fight for dollars with television, radio, newspapers, outdoor billboards, direct mail, online computer services. . . . The list is almost endless.

Once the magazine space has been agreed on, in terms of price, special features, and positioning, it is time to make the actual buy. At larger agencies this is accomplished through a Magazine Authorization, which sets out the terms of the contract to which both parties must agree. Some clients may like to see this first, to be sure they know what they are getting. If everyone accepts these terms, the media specialist can go ahead and authorize the buy.

Getting News into Newspapers

The purchase process for newspapers is similar to that of magazines. First, the buyer must analyze all possible newspapers available in each designated market, looking at factors such as circulation, coverage, audience composition, color possibilities, and zoning (the ability to customize ads to different areas of the paper's coverage area, or only appear in selected editions). Then, he or she must negotiate with each newspaper to obtain the best rate. Newspapers today are most often purchased in terms of Standard Ad Unit sizes, or SAUs, so that although the size of the newspaper itself may vary, the size of the ads within it are standardized. Just as with magazines, the newspaper buyer will usually want to specify where in the paper the ad will appear—an ad for salad dressing in the food section, a movie or restaurant ad in the entertainment section, and a furniture store ad in the home section. Sometimes, that decision is made based on what the target audience is more likely to read, so an ad for cellular phone service might appear in the business section, to reach professionals who are more likely to be interested in that item.

Once the deal has been negotiated and agreed upon, an insertion order is placed with the newspaper. At the same time, the agency will issue a Newspaper Authorization that sets out all of the specifications for the ad, such as whether it will be black and white or color, whether it includes a coupon or not, and any special instructions. Then all the print details must be confirmed, including the insertion dates, closing dates, ad size, column inches, inch rate, gross cost, contract rate, and position in the newspaper. This is done for every newspaper in which the ad will appear. After that has received approval, the insertion order goes ahead and the buy is made.

Buying Time on Television

There are three ways that national television is bought, for both broadcast and cable TV and syndication—long-term, short-term ("scatter"), and opportunistic. The first, and most intense, is what is generally known as the "upfront" marketplace. For broadcast TV this takes place in early to mid-June, while for cable, it follows shortly after in July. With either television form, the media specialist negotiates time with the major networks well in advance of the actual air dates. Most typically, these fall during the following TV season that starts in September and runs through to the following May. The time purchased is usually over three to four quarters of the year.

When you buy *long-term,* you receive a guaranteed rating, along with the opportunity to set up cancellation options. Typically, the options decelerate over the future quarters. For instance, in the first quarter, you might buy all of the spots confirmed; in the second quarter, three-quarters, or 75 percent might be firm, with the option to cancel the remaining 25 percent by an agreed-upon date. Then for the third or subsequent quarters, only half of the spots you negotiate are firm, and half (50 percent) are cancellable by a certain date. One advantage of buying time this way is that more favorable rates may be offered up front, as the networks like to lock in the advertisers to their shows (both new and returning series). Also, advertisers are more likely to get a better mix of programs, and to ensure they get their spots in the time periods and/or shows they want. The disadvantage, from the buyers' standpoint, is that there may be less room for negotiation because everyone is trying to buy from a limited amount of inventory. That is, the networks can choose how much of the available airtime they wish to sell up front, manipulating the demand for that time.

The commercial minutes the networks hold back or don't sell then form the bulk of the second type of national television time, which is known as the *scatter* market because it is scattered throughout the broadcast day across months. Buyers typically purchase this type of commercial time on a quarterly basis, usually two to three months in advance of the quarter, unless demand is soft. Prices in scatter will vary, depending on the supply and demand, and what happens in scatter tends to impact the long-term, or up-front marketplace, too. Up until 1990, advertiser demand during the up-front period was high, thanks in large part to the thriving U.S. economy, but when the recession hit the industry in 1990, advertisers were loathe to commit large funds in advance and so up-front deals decreased while scatter buys rose. For the next few years, long-term demand remained soft, and scatter rates climbed. In 1994, the picture changed somewhat again, with strong up-front sales returning as long-term deals looked increasingly favorable.

Advertisers who purchase spots in the scatter market may or may not get guaranteed ratings, depending on the demand. Those spots are usually cheaper, and give the buyer more flexibility rather than being locked in, for example, to appearing on "60 Minutes" every week for 12 months. If demand for scatter time is high, the network can "close" a particular daypart on very short notice, pulling it out of sale and then repricing it for future buyers. Advertisers who do not move quickly enough may find themselves shut out of the daypart completely.

Finally, the third way to buy time in national television is the *opportunistic* buy. Here, the advertiser chooses to purchase at the last minute, picking up whatever remains available. The advantage here is that the rates are usually most favorable to the buyer because the network wants to sell that time. The obvious drawback, however, is that there is less choice and little or no flexibility in the deal. Spots can be purchased as late as the day before airtime. Several sports events are sold this way.

Deciding how to purchase TV time depends on many factors, not the least of which is the size of the advertising budget. The number of quarters in which the commercial is to run plays a key role here too, as does the type of programming mix desired. First and foremost, however, should be strategic considerations regarding the impact of the decision on the marketing, advertising, and media goals.

How Television Time Is Bought

The way the process of buying television time works is as follows. The buyer requests a package of programs from the seller (broadcast, syndication, or cable). The package may be based on costs or on ratings. The sellers submit their inventory, and the buyer chooses the package that best meets the client's needs. Instead of purchasing them immediately, however, the buyer "goes to hold," which means the buyer is almost certain he or she will buy that time but has not fully committed to it yet. Both sides agree on how long that "hold" will last; generally, it is three to five days in the scatter market, and four to six weeks in the long-term market. After that period, the buyer will either purchase the time or drop out. Once the deal is finalized, however, the buyer effectively owns that time. If, later on, the buyer wants to get rid of the commercial time he or she bought, the network may try to sell it to a different advertiser, if the marketplace demand is strong. On the other hand, if for some reason the spot does not run as promised, the buyer is given the option of a comparable spot on the program schedule. This is known as a *make-good*. That might mean moving with a program to another day or time, if the network decides to reschedule it, or staying in the same daypart but switching programs.

All national television time is priced based on a 30-second spot. For advertisers wishing to buy more or less time than that, the rates are adjusted accordingly. Hence, a 60-second spot costs twice as much, and a 15-second spot is half the full rate. Negotiations are conducted based on costs-per-thousand, or CPMs.

Buying Time on Syndication and Cable

Buying national television time on syndication and cable is not that different from the broadcast network marketplace. That is, there are long-term, scatter, and opportunistic buys available in each television form. Additional considerations need to be given, however, to the individual buys. With syndication, for example, *coverage* is critical. Because syndicated programs are sold to individual stations in each market, they may not be seen in every market across the country. The buyer therefore has to know what percent of stations in the United States will air a given program. It may be as low as 60 percent, or as high as 99 percent. The day and/or time of airing will also vary by town or city, and although people do watch programs rather than dayparts, it may well make a difference to the effectiveness of a media schedule if you are trying to reach women 25 to 54 with "Oprah" and find that it airs at 9:00 A.M. in Chattanooga, Tennessee, but 3:00 P.M. in Gary, Indiana. The audience delivery and composition could be quite different in those markets because of that airtime variation.

Syndicated programs are guaranteed, but the syndicator almost always overstates the ratings estimate. That means the buyer then has to be given make-goods, either in the form of bonus units or cash back. While this may seem easy to resolve, the syndication market-place has been like this since its inception, and its strength is shown in the fact that not only is it continuing to grow, but much of the inventory is sold on a long-term basis.

Cable television also sells a good deal of its commercial time in advance, usually with guaranteed ratings. Those are not always available in the cable scatter market. Here, the variation tends to be by network. Cable is bought either by individual program or by rotation ("run of schedule"). Certain networks, such as Nick-at-Nite and MTV, only sell time in rotation, because there is strong enough advertiser demand for their units that they do not need to sell individual programs. While this might appear to be a big problem for advertisers, it is less critical on cable, where the programming is "vertical", and an advertiser knows that his spot will most likely air, for example, between music videos on MTV or in classic sitcoms on Nick-at-Nite.

Local TV and Radio Buys

The purchase of time on spot television and spot radio has both similarities and differences to the network process. Local television buyers usually buy time on shorter notice than for national television. They also have to deal with individual stations in each market, rather than buying a complete network, unless they make a buy across various stations that are linked together into an ad sales network. The planner provides the buyer with the details of the specifications, which include the marketing and media objectives, a demographic and psychographic description of the target, the desired dayparts and flights, the number of ratings points per market and/or time period, the total budget, and the mix of commercial lengths (:15s, :30s, and :60s).

Armed with this information, the buyer can then start negotiating with stations in those markets. Rather than discuss the cost of an individual spot or the cost per thousand used in national television buys, both of which will vary considerably by market, buyers typically negotiate the cost per rating point, or CPP. That way, they ensure that the appropriate number of rating points are purchased, at or below the amount budgeted. The negotiating process is quite subtle. The buyer does not want the seller to know how much money is available (as the station would want to get all of it!), and the seller does not want the buyer to know how much inventory is available (as that would let the buyer know how low a price he or she could get). The buyer will usually talk to all of the stations in the market that have programs or formats appropriate for the target in the desired daypart and ask each of them to submit prices. For some advertisers, price is the most important criterion, so the buyer looks to purchase "tonnage"—lots of media weight at the lowest price available. For others, the program or format is key; they may be willing to pay slightly more to get a closer fit between target and vehicle. It depends on the strategy outlined in the media plan.

Once the buyer has received submissions from each station, he or she can then start negotiating to see if any of the sellers are willing to lower their price any further. While this used to take several days or even weeks, in today's competitive climate buyers are less likely to give the stations much time to come in with a lower bid, and will usually decide fairly quickly which stations to purchase. Having made that decision, the final prices and terms are agreed to and the buy is made.

In theory, local television and radio buys are fixed; that is, the time is bought on a given daypart and/or program (unless the buyer purchases "run-of-schedule," or ROS, which means that the station can air the spot at any time). In practice, however, stations may well pre-empt a spot if another advertiser comes in who is willing to pay more for that time slot. If this happens, the first advertiser will usually request a make-good or compensation if the station airs his spot at a less favorable time.

While buying local radio is similar in many respects to buying television, there are two opportunities for advertisers that are commonly made available in the audio medium. The first is merchandising and promotions. This has become an extremely important consideration for many companies that use spot radio, particularly national advertisers. Local radio stations may be willing, as part of the deal, to run special contests for listeners or set up a remote site broadcast or hold a special event for the trade, for example. The Buick car dealership could offer a new car as the grand prize in an on-air contest; the afternoon music show could be aired from the dealer's showroom, or a cocktail reception for all new Buick owners could be held at the radio station one evening. Such promotions need to be negotiated as part of the buy, but they may add considerably to the efficiency of the purchase.

The second difference that local radio can offer advertisers is the chance for live commercials. In the earliest days of radio, all commercials were spoken live by announcers on-air. Today, that is only possible at the local-market level. Some advertisers believe that having a local radio personality deliver the message adds greater authority and credibility to the product, giving it an implied endorsement. While this is not in fact true (the station never officially endorses any individual brand), it can be beneficial for the advertiser. In addition, because relatively few commercials are presented this way anymore, if offers you another way to stand out from the crowd.

The Great Outdoors

Because outdoor billboards are bought on a market-by-market basis, the buying process is, in some ways, similar to local TV and radio buying. Here, instead of dealing with individual TV or radio stations (or rep firms that put stations together into a network), the media buyer must either deal with individual outdoor plant operators, or with networks of plants that are available through large outdoor companies such as Gannett Outdoor or Patrick Media Group.

Negotiations for outdoor billboards focus on several key elements: size, location, showing, and cost/CPM. The first criterion to consider is the poster or panel size—from an 8-sheet to a painted bulletin. As explained in Chapter 4, different boards are purchased for different timeframes, with posters typically being sold on a 30-day basis and bulletins sold in a much longer-term deal, such as six months or one year.

Location is really the key as far as outdoor is concerned. For certain products, such as a local restaurant, you might want to be on smaller posters in the city to remind people of your address; for hotels or gas stations, highways would make more sense, to reach drivers as they are passing through your area. It is important, too, to know which side of the street the board is located (the right side is preferable), and whether there are any potential blockages that could get in the line of sight for the board, such as a tall building or tree. This kind of information can best be gained by actually going to the location to look at the board. The operator can provide you with a complete inventory of addresses for both bulletins and poster panels. In the case of posters, you can also find out if the poster is in an ethnic neighborhood and/or restricted location (no alcohol or tobacco), and whether it is on a wall or a pole.

The outdoor showing that you buy will tell you what the number of daily exposures are to your message as a percentage of the total market size. A #100 showing, therefore, means that 100 percent of the audience will pass that board in a 30-day period; a #50 means 50 percent will do so, and so on. Showings are calculated based on traffic patterns, however, which means that not everyone who physically goes by the location will necessarily see your ad (just as a TV program rating does not mean the viewer will watch your commercial). Poster panels are generally bought at the 25, 50, or 100 showing level, whereas bulletins are purchased at 5, 10 or 15 showing increments. Each showing size in a market will have associated with it the number of poster panels utilized. This is known as the *allotment.*

Last, but not least, comes the cost of the buy. Outdoor is bought and sold on the basis of the cost of reaching 1,000 of the target audience, or CPM. Unlike TV or radio, though, there are usually only a few operators to choose from in a given market, which limits the flexibility that the buyer has to negotiate. And it is often the case that where there is more than one company to choose from, one will have better locations for a particular size board, while the other will have better offerings in a different size or location.

Once all of the negotiations have taken place, the media specialist will issue an outdoor authorization, laying out all of the details, or specifications, of the buy. These are then confirmed with the client and the seller, and the purchase can proceed.

Summary

Even the most impressive media plan will not achieve its goals if the buys are not made effectively. That means the time and space need to be purchased in accordance with the plan's specifications, in terms of criteria such as timing, ad size, and placement or position within the media vehicle. For magazines and newspapers, editorial adjacencies may be key, so that the ad message is seen in an appropriate context, such as an ad for cellular phone service targeting business people in the Business section of a newspaper or a wrinkle cream targeting women in the Beauty section of a particular magazine. The costs for print media may be negotiable, off the rate card, depending on the competitiveness of the magazine category.

Buying time on electronic media is always done through negotiations, either with a network or individual stations. TV buys may be long-term (purchased up-front) or short-term (in the scatter market). The guarantees and costs of those buys will vary accordingly. For radio, where most time is purchased locally, buyers deal with stations or rep firms that sell them a package of stations across the markets in which the buyer is interested. Deals are usually made based on the cost per rating point. For outdoor billboards, the key buying criterion to consider is the location of the board, whether a poster or a bulletin. Buyers negotiate the cost to reach a given proportion of the market, estimated using showings. The process can be handled with individual plant operators or through networks.

Checklist—Making the Media Buys

1. Do you have all the necessary specifications regarding the objectives, the target audience, vehicle preferences, GRP needs, and budget limitations to proceed to the buys?
2. Does the client have to approve the buys before they are finalized?

3. For magazines, is a discount available for a volume buy?

4. Do you want a preferred position for your magazine ad?

5. Are you trying to reach a more specialized or generalized audience with magazines (priced accordingly)?

6. Are any special promotions, editorial features, bonus circulation, or trade deals being offered by any of the magazines?

7. Do you want your newspaper ad to appear in a special section?

8. Are there any special instructions needed for your newspaper ad, such as a coupon or inclusion of color?

9. Do you want to buy time on network, cable, or syndicated TV?

10. Is your national television buy going to be made for the long-term (up-front) or short-term (scatter)?

11. Can you get ratings guarantees for your national TV buy?

12. For a syndicated TV buy, what is your clearance?

13. With a cable TV buy, do you want a specific time period or will a rotation suffice?

14. For a local TV buy, is media weight (tonnage) more important than specific program selection?

15. For local radio or local TV, do you want to deal directly with each station, or do you prefer to use a rep firm?

16. Are your outdoor billboards' locations satisfactory?

17. Do you have enough billboards in each market to generate sufficient showings?

CHAPTER NINE

Evaluating the Media Plan

O ne of the most often-repeated quotations about advertising was attributed to Lord Leverhulme, founder of the Lever Brothers Company, who said that he knew half of the money he spent on advertising was wasted; he just didn't know which half. Your job, as a media specialist, is to try to ensure that your client's dollars are not wasted. One way to achieve that is by evaluating the media plan before it is executed, and then again once it is up and running.

It is no longer true that an annual plan is left unchanged for a whole year; more and more, advertisers will make changes to at least some part of the marketing plan while the campaign is running. This may be in response to changes in any part of the marketing mix. Consumer response could end up being greater or less than anticipated; product improvements could necessitate additional promotional efforts; new channels of distribution could become important;

or competitive pricing strategies may require alterations to the original, approved plan. And beyond that, economic trends can affect almost all marketing efforts. For example, in the early 1990s, most "experts" predicted that the economic recession would be over soon, suggesting that consumer spending would improve. What in fact happened was that consumer confidence in the economy remained low, leading people to continue their restrained purchasing habits. This had a marked effect on the manufacturers of high-ticket items such as stereos and electronics. It also impacted general eating habits, causing people to eat out less and stay home more.

This chapter presents two of the ways that a media plan can be evaluated, before and after it begins running. We have explained the concepts of reach and frequency. With today's sophisticated computer programs, syndicated data on past purchase and media consumption can be analyzed to give a "best guess" estimate of how well a medium, or total plan, will reach the chosen target audience. This can later be compared with actual results on reach and frequency, to see how well the plan actually performed, which is crucial information for preparing next year's plan. The second type of evaluation is to check that your ads actually run as scheduled, a practice known as post-buy analysis. It is up to the media specialist to make sure that if, for some reason, the ad did not run as scheduled or was not positioned in the agreed-upon place, that some form of compensation is given, either monetary or in time or space.

Pre-Plan Analysis

The first time to evaluate the impact of the media plan is before it is presented to the client. That is, in selecting the media vehicles you think will best meet the advertising and marketing objectives, the media specialist needs to figure out which combination of vehicles will do the best job of reaching the target an acceptable number of times. Computer programs are readily available to help make these kinds of analyses simple and fast.

For example, let's say you were considering two alternative combinations for your media plan for the Super-Kleen cleanser. The first combination would use monthly insertions in *Home* magazine, along with periodic commercials in prime time on cable television. Another possibility would be to place continuous messages on cable, with occasional ads in the magazine. Here is how the two schedules might look for the year:

Schedule One	Schedule Two
12 insertions in "Home" (53 GRPs)	4 insertions in "Home" (18 GRPs)
400 GRPs in Primetime Cable	1,000 GRPs in Primetime Cable

And here is how the two schedules would perform against your target of women 25 to 54:

	Schedule One	Schedule Two
Total GRPs	453	1,018
Reach 1+	50.7%	50.3%
Reach 3+	54.2%	52.5%
Frequency	8.4	18.8

So, even though you are using far more cable in Schedule Two, the impact on the overall reach is actually less than if you used more magazine advertising, as in Schedule One.

Post-Buy Analysis

What the media specialist must find out once the plan is running is whether the ads ran as scheduled, and how well the plan actually delivered. For the first part, determining that the ads did in fact run as scheduled, you can turn to various sources, depending on the medium. For newspapers, there are *tear sheets,* which are provided by commercial services, to show you examples of the actual ad in the newspaper. Magazines will usually provide copies of the issues in which your ad appears. For television and radio, you should receive affidavits confirming when your spot aired. In each case, the media specialist must check that the terms of the contract were adhered to. If you requested being in the food section of the paper, or the first third of the magazine, is that where your ad was placed?

For broadcast media, the task is usually more complicated because program schedules are far more prone to being changed. You might have arranged for your radio spot to air between 6:00 P.M. and 8:00 P.M., only to find that it came on at 5:30 P.M. or 8:20 P.M.. Or, you could have bought a rotation of spots (ROS, or Run of Schedule), which in theory means that your spots will run in all dayparts. In analyzing the affidavits you might discover that more than half of the messages were aired between midnight and 6:00 A.M., or some other inappropriate time. It is then incumbent upon the station to explain what happened and, in all likelihood, offer some type of make-good, either in the form of free ads or financial compensation for the cost differences between ROS and the overnight period.

In larger agencies or organizations, this post-analysis checking is typically done by the media buyers or business service department. It is more of an accounting than a media function, but ultimately, the media specialist should know what happened, and why.

Later on, additional information becomes available to show how your ad schedule delivered. This is in the form of syndicated data, such as Nielsen for television, Arbitron for radio, and Mediamark Research, Inc. (MRI) or Simmons Market Research Bureau (SMRB) for print media. Each service provides the ratings and audience delivery of media vehicles to help you determine whether, in fact, you met the goals of your plan. Other companies can access this data also, acting as third-party vendors of the information.

The kinds of questions the data can help you answer include what percentage of the target was reached by the media (and vehicles) that you used (reach), and how often, on average, was the target exposed to them? It is worth emphasizing again that these terms refer only to media exposure, and not to actual exposure to the ads themselves. They should therefore be thought of as *opportunities to see* your message. Many advertisers will discount, or "weight" the exposure levels to account for this distinction, assuming, for example, that only half of the people reached by the media vehicle will actually see the ad. Or they may only look at the proportion of the target that is exposed a certain number of times (*effective reach*), assuming here that people will require several opportunities to see your message before they in fact will do so.

The importance of evaluating the plan once it has gone into effect cannot be underestimated. For only by doing so will you find out, first, whether you got what you (or your client) paid for, and second, whether the plan worked as you intended. It will provide invaluable help in preparing for next year's plan, too. Although, ultimately, the impact of the media plan, and the other elements of the marketing mix, is determined at the cash register, it is helpful to be able to analyze the individual parts to find out what is, or is not, working. Having said that, and acknowledging the truth to this chapter's opening comment by Lord Leverhulme, you should keep in mind that it is difficult to determine the precise effect of advertising media messages on consumers. We know *when* it is working, though we may not always know *how*.

Yet, without evaluating how a media plan performs, we are left even more in the dark than when we began. In effect, it means that each time we create a plan, we end up recreating the wheel. This can lead you down two paths. Either the same plan is reproduced because it "seemed to work" (or at least, didn't cause any disasters). Or the plan is completely changed to see if that makes a difference in sales, or awareness, or attitudes. Both of these options are flawed. To continue doing exactly the same thing as before without knowing whether it is working, or if it could possibly be improved upon, is detrimental to your product (and client), keeping them from performing at their best. Similarly, to overturn the plan without analyzing how it worked (or didn't work) means that you run the risk of losing the momentum your ads might have started to build, and jeopardizes your chances for success.

So although there is a strong temptation, once the media plan is completed and the ads are running, to file it away and move on to the next stage, the true media specialist will carry on the task through to the end. He or she is responsible for ensuring not only that the ads run as intended, but that they delivered what was planned. If these two evaluation tasks are carried out successfully, you will not only have a more satisfied client, but will have already taken an important step forward in preparing for next year's media plan.

Summary

A completed media plan is really not final until it has been evaluated to see how it has performed. This should be done both before the plan is executed, by calculating estimates of reach and frequency that the plan should achieve, and afterwards, through post-buy analyses to ensure that the ads ran as scheduled. If the messages did not air as intended and specified in the buys, it is up to the media specialist to obtain some type of compensation. Without these checks, there is no way of knowing whether this year's plan should be continued into the following year with or without modifications. And, although it is always difficult to pinpoint precisely the impact of advertising on sales, the process of evaluating the success or failure of the media plan in achieving the media, advertising, and marketing objectives will help the brand and the client know how to do better next year.

Checklist—Evaluating the Media Plan

1. Have you performed reach and frequency analyses of the media plan before presenting it to the client?
2. Have you contacted clipping services or the print media themselves to determine that your ads ran as scheduled?
3. Are the post-buys for electronic media available to ensure that your ads ran as scheduled?
4. Do you have access to syndicated data such as Nielsen, Arbitron, MRI, and SMRB, for future analysis of how your media vehicles performed against your target?
5. Do you have ideas on how your media plan can be improved for next year?

APPENDIX A

Key Resources

Advertising Age
740 N. Rush Street
Chicago, IL 60611
Weekly trade magazine covering
the advertising industry.

Advertising Research Foundation
641 Lexington Avenue
New York NY 10022
Industry-wide, not-for-profit
association dedicated to
increasing the effectiveness of
advertising.

Adweek
Weekly trade magazine covering
the advertising industry.

American Demographics
127 W. State Street, PO Box 68,
Ithaca, NY 14850
Publisher of American
Demographics magazine, a
monthly publication dedicated to
tracking and analyzing consumer
trends.

The Arbitron Company
142 West 57th Street
New York NY 10019
Provides local radio audience
measurement data on a
subscription basis.

ASI Market Research
79 Fifth Avenue
New York, NY 10003
Research company involved in
brand equity analysis, advertising
response modeling, and natural,
in-theater copytesting.

Audits & Surveys
The Audits & Surveys Building
650 Avenue of the Americas
New York NY 10011
Marketing research organization
that offers consumer, media,
financial and advertising
effectiveness research.

Audit Bureau of Circulation
900 North Meacham Road
Schaumburg, IL 60173
Auditing body of the magazine
and newspaper industries.
Assesses circulation on a
six-month basis.

Broadcast Data Systems
1515 Broadway
New York NY 10036
Pattern recognition system
used to monitor TV and radio
commercials and programs to
provide media verification
and competitive analysis
services.

Bruskin/Goldring Research, Inc.
100 Metroplex Drive
Edison, NJ 08817
Consumer research company
involved in large-scale studies of
attitudes, opinions, and behavior.

Claritas/NPDC
20 Terrace Hill
Ithaca, NY 14851
Marketing and demographic
information based on
geodemographic analysis and
mapping using the Compass
system.

Competitive Media Reporting
11 West 42nd Street
New York, NY 10036
Joint venture of Leading National
Advertisers (LNA) and Arbitron,
providing competitive media
expenditures for 11 media via
monthly volumes and/or software.

Donovan Data Systems
115 West 18th Street
New York, NY 10011
Provides online access to Nielsen
TV and Arbitron radio
information, for pre-buy process
and audience analysis, as well as
for payments and invoicing.

Gallup and Robinson
575 Ewing Street
Princeton, NJ 08540
Research company offering TV
commercial testing service, as
well as public opinion survey
research.

Information Resources, Inc.
150 North Clinton Street
Chicago, IL 60661
Array of marketing research services, including new product testing, marketing mix testing, product tracking, promotion evaluation, and computerized decision support services.

Interactive Market Systems, Inc. (IMS)
11 West 42nd Street, 11th Floor
New York, NY 10036
Software for media planning and market analysis.

Marketing Resources Plus
555 Twin Dolphin Drive
Redwood City, CA 94065
Software for media planning and buying, particularly for local market analysis.

Mediamark Research Inc.
708 Third Avenue, 8th Floor
New York, NY 10017
Syndicated research on media and product usage, along with supporting software systems for analysis. Also conducts biannual study on teenagers, and permits importation of other custom or syndicated databases.

Monroe Mendelsohn Research
841 Broadway
New York, NY 10003
Marketing and media research on the affluent consumer.

Nielsen Marketing Research
Nielsen Plaza
Northbrook, IL 60062
Offers array of information and data services to plan, test and evaluate all elements of a marketing program. The Household Services division operates a 40,000 in-home consumer panel to measure purchase behavior.

Nielsen Media Research
299 Park Avenue
New York, NY 10171
Provides national and local television audience measurement data on a subscription basis.

Nustats, Inc.
901 West Martin Luther King
Austin, TX 78701
Provides Hispanic Info source national syndicated study of U.S. Hispanic adults.

J.D. Power and Associates
30401 Agoura Road
Agoura Hills, CA 91301
Survey research company specializing in automotive and travel industries.

The Pretesting Company
38 Franklin Street
Tenafly, NJ 07670
Offers pretesting of TV, radio, print and outdoor advertisements in laboratory condition. Eye-tracking diagnostics available also.

Roper Starch Worldwide
205 East 42nd Street
New York, NY 10017

Roper division provides comprehensive survey research on attitudes, opinions, and behavior. Starch division offers analysis of magazine advertising effectiveness.

Scarborough Research Corporation
11 West 42nd Street
New York, NY 10036

Single source media, consumer and demographic syndicated surveys in the top 50 local markets. Primary emphasis is on newspaper readership, but other media and product usage included too.

Simmons Market Research Bureau
420 Lexington Avenue
New York NY 10170

Syndicated research on media and product usage, along with supporting software systems for analysis. Also conducts biannual studies on children and teenagers, and new annual studies of Hispanics and African-Americans.

Standard Rate & Data Service
2000 Clearwater Drive
Oak Brook, IL 60521

Provides cost information on all major media.

Strategy Research Corporation
100 NW 37th Avenue
Miami, FL 33125

Primary emphasis on the Hispanic consumer, measuring product and media usage.

Tapscan
3000 Riverchase Galleria
Suite 850
Birmingham, AL 35244

Software for planning and buying of all major media.

Telmar
902 Broadway
New York, NY 10010

Marketing, media planning and flowcharting software.

VMI Viewfacts
70 West Madison Street,
Suite 800
Chicago, IL 60602

Measurement system to measure on moment-by-moment basis consumer response to commercials.

Yankelovich Partners
Eight Wright Street
Westport, CT 06880

Marketing research and public opinion company.

APPENDIX B

Associations
and Sources

Associations

Advertiser Syndicated Television
Association
1756 Broadway
Suite 3J
New York, NY 10019

American Association of
Advertising Agencies
666 Third Avenue
13th Floor
New York, NY 10017

Association of National
Advertisers
155 East 44th Street
New York, MY 10017

Cabletelevision Advertising
Bureau
757 Third Avenue
5th Floor
New York, NY 10017

Electronic Media Rating Council
509 Madison Avenue, Suite 1112
New York, NY 10022

Magazine Publishers of America
575 Lexington Avenue
New York, NY 10022

National Association of
Broadcasters
1771 N Street, N.W.
Washington, DC 20036

Network Television Association
825 Seventh Avenue
4th Floor
New York, NY 10019

Newspaper Association of
America
1180 Avenue of the Americas
New York, NY 10036

Point of Purchase Advertising
Institute
66 North Van Brunt Street
Englewood, NJ 07631

Radio Advertising Bureau
304 Park Avenue South
7th Floor
New York, NY 10010

Television Bureau of Advertising
477 Madison Avenue
New York, NY 10022

Traffic Audit Bureau
114 East 32nd Street
Suite 802
New York, NY 10016

Yellow Pages Publishers
Association
820 Kirts Boulevard
Suite 100
Troy, MI 48084

Sources

Willam D. Wells, *Planning for R.O.I.: Effective Advertising Strategy*. Englewood Cliffs, NJ: Prentice Hall, 1989.

Samir Husni, *Samir Husni's Guide to New Consumer Magazines*, Volume 8, 1993. Folio Press.

Herbert E. Krugman. "The Impact of Television Advertising: Learning Without Involvement," *Public Opinion Quarterly*, Volume 29, 349–356.

Index

TITLES OF INTEREST IN
PRINT AND BROADCAST MEDIA

For further information or a current catalog, write:
NTC Business Books
a division of *NTC Publishing Group*
4255 West Touhy Avenue
Lincolnwood, Illinois 60646–1975